Character Development

as

Spiritual Transformation

A Writer's Guide

by

Push Hardly

First Edition

Press Hardly

Columbus OH

presshardly.com

ISBN 978-0-9909156-0-7

This book has little to do

With spiritualism,

Or spirituality.

Not directly anyway.

Not unless you want it to.

To:

G. A. L.

Character Development

As

Spiritual Transformation

A Writer's Guide

By Push Hardly

Author's Note

There are many ways to present a character developing throughout a story. Each method has its merits based upon the type of story being told. The type of character development discussed in this book involves a development that appears to the audience as more of a spiritual transformation.

The term 'spiritual transformation' carries a lot of meaning. Often it conjures ideas of finding God, or opening one's mind to the interconnectedness of the Universe. Spiritual transformation ultimately means a significant change in the way the world is perceived, and reacted to. When Spiritual transformation is shown through character development, it is presented as a cathartic and deeply personal transformation, whereby the character's entire outlook is altered by the end of the story.

Of course, the characters in a story are not real people, so they cannot actually experience a spiritual transformation. This is important to keep in mind because, in spite of this, the audience will need to believe the character is real, and believe the character has had such a transformation.

True spiritual transformation among actual people is a deeply internal experience. Powerful ideas and personal interpretation of experiences take place, which are difficult to express outwardly. Showing such a transformation happening in a fictional character forces storytellers to use story elements that will act as a substitution for the internal experiences an audience expects to occur in a spiritual transformation.

The goal of this book is to establish a set of storytelling tools, and to present stages of character development, which used together can help create a meaningful sense of connection the audience feels towards a character. These will allow the story to reveal what is happening inside a character's head without explicitly stating it. In this way, an audience can add their own introspection, making the experience of the audience all the more personal and powerful.

Presenting the spiritual transformation of a character involves understanding many things about human nature, about writing, about the audience, and about building a character. A story teller must understand how an audience thinks, and why they think that way. To discuss so many different things requires this book to weave through a maze of topics.

While the premiss of this book is to provide a storyteller a sense of order for creating stories, there is a bit of jumping around topics in this book. In an attempt to organize what might seem as unorganized thoughts, this book is set into four different sections.

The first section establishes the starting point for creating a character who will experience a spiritual transformation, that is to say, it lays out the need for a character to start the story in a place of denial. The first section explores why a character will be in this state of denial, so that the audience can relate to it. This section will list requirements for creating the world in which a character lives, and other elements of creating that character. It will cover her talents, desires, and creating the world in which she lives.

The second section delves into philosophical reasons for several of the approaches presented in this book. There are some old ideas presented with perhaps fresh reasoning. Hopefully you will find other ideas new and interesting.

The third section briefly lays out a series of stages a story outline could include to present a character experiencing a spiritual transformation. While these are presented as stages, each story will have its own requirements for which stages are used.

The fourth section is a short story written to demonstrate the ideas presented in this book. It was written after the first draft of this book was completed as a proof of concept. This section, and the book, closes with a discussion of that story.

There are some genres of stories where character development is not an important part of the story, such as a series, or where the main character has a story problem, and not an internal problem. However, under-standing the ideas in this book may help improve such stories, as there are ideas in this book that are useful for any storyteller.

In this book, the subject of a story (the main character) is referred to as a character, and as a hero. The feminine pronoun Her and She are used instead of the traditional His and He, or the more modern Them or Their. This happens only when talking about the main character of a story.

This book is directed to storytellers of all sorts: writers of books or short stories, those who script out movies and plays, and to those who relate spoken tales. The term audience is used to denote any group of people receiving the story; listeners, readers, or spectators.

This book is as short as I could possibly make it.

Foundations of Denial

Stories are built upon conflict. Storytellers use any number of tricks to generate conflict. Lies are common. Good vs evil is pervasive. The most interesting and captivating conflict arise when a character is in a state of conflict with herself. A self-conflict that stems from a denial of something about herself. Conflicts that originate from a character in a state of denial can propel the conflicts the hero has with other characters. It can drive the plot forward. It all starts with this.

A favorite joke goes like this.

A man goes to see his doctor. He is called in, and sits on the table. The man says, "Doctor. I'm feeling really agitated. Everybody plays this trick on me. They whisper all the time and I can't hear what they're saying. I get so angry, and I don't know what to do. I need something to calm me down."
The doctor cups his hands around his mouth, and yells, "Have you considered a hearing aid?"

In this joke, the man cannot accept that he is flawed, that his hearing is fading. He blames other people for his inability to hear what they are saying. The conflict originates with his denial that he is imperfect. The joke even suggests conflict exists between him and his family and friends, when he blames them for whispering. He blames other people for his flaw.

When telling a story, the character can be shown in a similar state of denial. She can be introduced to the idea that she is not perfect. The story can then get the audience to witness and understand the character is flawed, and show her in a state of denial.

Eventually, the story will force the character to realize that she is flawed. The character will struggle to improve, until she will accept her flaw. Then her real work begins.

The idea of a hero is one of a super-being who is always great. Sometimes she might possess a dark side, or bear complex emotions. These can make fun stories that are centered around action. It's a common way to present backstory. However, this is a poor medium to demonstrate character development. Instead, consider creating an 'Imperfect Hero'.

An imperfect hero will think she is great, but she will have flaws. She will refuse to admit having any flaws. She must struggle to come to terms with these flaws. She eventually will overcome them, and succeed. She becomes a true hero at the end of the story because she is willing to take on the most difficult challenge; herself.

The imperfect hero will resist change to show the audience her denial. How conflict with others manifests during the story must reflect the conflict that exists within herself. This is the true reason conflict exists between two characters in a story. Conflict is a tool that demonstrates the character's internal conflict. Artificial conflict, that exists between characters without this foundation, can be kind of boring.

To create great stories we have to start by building our imperfect hero. We need to build the character from the ground up. I mean that in a literal way, well literarily. First we have to build the ground they walk on. We need to create a world, one with a flaw, and a joy.

The World's Flaw & Joy

This chapter will discuss building a world with a flaw, and a joy. There is also attention to how the people in this world behave. These will help shape the character when it comes to creating her. It may help some to write down ideas generated with questions presented below.

To create a character who can experience a spiritual transformation the story must first establish a reason her flaw exists. The world flaw gives unspoken support for her flaw, and prevents her from coming off as annoying. For example, an unhappy character in a world of plenty runs the risk of sounding like a spoiled brat. However, if the world is flawed (perhaps people are exposed to lots of advertising) such a character's responses appear to be more reasonable.

When a character has a flawed behavior that is the result of the world's flaw, the character's flaw becomes much more believable. It creates reasonable deniability.

Reasonable deniability is something in the world that explains why a flaw (or other story element) might exist. It provides some basis for the character to reasonably deny that she has a flaw. The story must quickly provide subtle explanations for the character's flawed behavior to exist, and show the world is flawed. She has an subconscious 'excuse' for her flawed behavior to exist.

A world flaw cannot exist without a world. So, first, one must understand what a world is. A 'world' doesn't have to be an entire planet, although it could be. A world is the immediate environment in which the character acts, and reacts, on a daily basis, i.e. a city, a neighborhood, a school, an office, outer-space. All of these could provide the boundaries necessary for her 'world' to exist.

Examples of worlds and flaws: A neighborhood where cars drive too fast, a futuristic city filled with aggressive automatons, an office full of cubicles that is ruled by an uncaring boss, a small town.

The character must be from this world. She must be part of this world. She must have a shared past with it.

Stories that introduce a character to a new world have problems demonstrating character development. Examples of this might include time travel, exploring the depths of the ocean, space marines fighting aliens. These scenarios have limited opportunities for spiritual transformation, because these characters have been thrust into a world that did not mold who they are as a person.

This is not spiritual growth, it is self discovery. This can be an exciting element in a story, but unless this new world is somehow part of the character's history, the character will not resist change, and thus will not experience a spiritual transformation.

There are ways to make any world part of the character's history. The time traveller might be returning to her childhood home. Perhaps a marine lives in space and battles aliens often. Perhaps the ocean explorer used to scuba dive with her mother. A shared history with a place allows for spiritual flaws to have been established between the character and the world.

Once we have an idea of our world and its flaw, we must also create how the typical inhabitants respond to this world, how they live and act. Typical means stereotypical.

A typical response is important, because it can shape how the main character acts and responds during the story, either in coordination with, or in opposition to, the other inhabitants of the world.

For example, typical people living in the Western part of the United States of America, during the 1800s, might be God- fearing, strong-willed people, who fight bandits, and deal with American Indians. If your world is inner-city Chicago during the 1930s, people will typically struggle to keep their families safe from crime, and the Depression, while slipping out to enjoy alcohol at a speakeasy. If your typical people are fish who live on a reef, perhaps they all send their kids to fish-school, like in the movie <u>Nemo</u>.

At this point you may wish to stop and write two sentences. In the first sentence, briefly describe a world and its flaw. In the next sentence, write the typical inhabitant's response to this world and flaw. As new ideas about worlds and flaws come to you, write them down as well, then keep moving forward.

Your sentences might look something like this:

World - A bakery with tasty foods, overseen by an irate chef who is obsessive about cleanliness.

Response - A typical person in the bakery will be tempted by the baked goods, yet fearful of making a mess and enraging the chef.

The two sentences give definition to our world, and some behavioral requirements are automatically placed upon any character who might live in this world. Even before we begin to imagine her, we get a sense of how we might expect a main character to behave. She might adore the chef, or behave completely differently - perhaps she does not like sweets, or could be uncaring about cleanliness.

With these two sentences we have a starting place to define our character and her spiritual transformation. Slow down on creating a flawed character, just yet. There is more to do before we create our imperfect hero.

World Joy

Every world must possess a joy, something that is free of all conflict. The world joy is revealed to the audience through an action. It is rarely explained, and preferably witnessed or experienced with little dialogue. It is something of simple pleasure, such as a sunset, or a bike ride. The imperfect hero is not able to experience the world joy. But the audience must know that it exists.

The world joy exists for reasons that will be explained in a later chapter. You don't need to create world joy yet, but keep in mind your world will need one.

Avoid making the world joy something the hero desires, such as holding hands. This approach limits the story potential. It is more compelling if the hero is oblivious to the world joy until they experience a spiritual transformation.

Later, this book will also cover desire. Holding hands could be an example of something the hero desires, but it should not also be the world joy. Find a world joy that is different from what is desired, and the story will have more power.

The world joy is a moment of value that is somewhat rare, or brief. It is the only thing in your story that has no conflict. It should be shown early in the story to prime the audience that it exists. It will most likely be shown through another character experiencing the world joy.

It is not quite time to create a character. Your world needs something else. A danger.

World Danger

The story needs a world danger. The entire basis of character development as spiritual transformation is built on a premiss that the character denies she has any flaws.

Real people can relate to this denial. When pushed, nearly all of us are willing to admit that we are flawed. One may have trouble correcting our flaws, like a smoker who laments an addiction, but can't quit cigarettes.

Admitting flaws demonstrates rational thought. It shows that we can see ourselves as others see us. We can speak about our flaws and diminish the power they have over us.

The character in a story will not be able admit her flaw. She won't even be able to speak about it. This is a severe level of avoidance, which must be addressed as a story element.

In any story, an audience will be asked to suspend belief. Suspending belief is based on the idea that in any story, something extraordinary can happen, but for the audience to accept such extraordinary elements they must first suspend what they expect to happen in the real world, and believe such things are possible in the world in which your story takes place. Suspending belief allows the fantastic to exist in a story. However, we must treat the audience's willingness to suspend belief with respect. This is why we have a world danger.

When the charter avoids admitting her flaw, the audience again comes to doubt anyone could be so blind, so stupid. The story should have already attempted to sooth the audience by tying the flaws of the character to the flaws of the world. However, if the character continues to deny having any flaws, the audience could be at risk of doubting the authenticity of the character's responses. They will have trouble suspending belief.

Even though the audience may experience this on a subconscious level, we should not take it lightly. The story must have a tool that exists to sooth this doubt in the audience. Something in the story will need to take the place of her failure to admit she has a flaw. This tool is the world danger.

The world danger is something that exists in the story that will act when the character demonstrates her flaw, and/or her unwillingness to admit her flaw exists. The world danger is the personification of her denial.

This world danger could be as life-threatening as a monster, or as common day as a cat who hisses at the hero on her way home from school. The world danger should relate to the character's flaw in some way.

There are things that the world danger is not. It is not the anti-hero. It is not the nemesis / arch-enemy. The world danger is not the main problem the hero fights against throughout the story. It is not a plot element. It might drive the character toward a plot point, but is not the plot in itself.

The world danger does exist throughout the story, right from the beginning. It acts at odds with the hero. However, it is only a metaphorical embodiment of the character's denial.

The external plot should be independent of this danger. The two exist for entirely different reasons. The plot exists to push the character towards spiritual transformation. The danger exists to establish that the hero has yet to spiritually transform. The plot and the world danger work together to ensure that the character completes the transformation.

To the character, the world-danger can be a validation of the flaw. That is, it can be proof in the character's mind that she is right in holding onto her flaw. Let's suppose the character's flaw is her thinking sidewalks are unsafe. If she encounter's a hissing cat on the way home from school, her flaw is validated, when really, it's just a cat.

A symbiotic relationship exists between the hero and the world danger. By relationship I mean just that. The hero and the world-danger should have a familiarity with each other.

There are symbolic reasons for having the world danger, which go beyond representing the character's denial of any flaw. If presented correctly, and tied to the world flaw, the world danger represents how people try to look at a symptom of a problem, instead of defining the underlying reasons about why a problem exists. The result is, the hero responds to the world-danger through conflict, or avoidance, and she does not tackle the internal problem (the flaw).

There is yet more symbology associated with the world danger. It represents the power fear has over our lives. It can drive us to ways of thinking that are closed minded.

Fear can be debilitating, preventing us from accepting truths. Fear can blind us to what is true, and this can also allow the audience to understand why a character continually denies her flaws. This helps the audience suspend belief about the character's denial.

The world danger need not be deadly. It could be the threat of being fired from a job. It could be a divorced parent's annoying new partner. Whatever the danger, it must show up early in the story, and appear at opportune moments.

Later, in the chapter Aftermath, the world danger will be revisited for discussion about taming the world danger, and how that expresses a completion of the hero's spiritual transformation.

If you have any thoughts of a world danger at this point add it to your list of sentences. Otherwise, think about how a world danger might fit in with your flawed world as you read further chapters.

The Flawed Body & Talent

We are getting closer to creating a character with a flaw. Before we do that, this chapter will cover creating other parts of a character, something about their body that offers definition, and we must give them a talent, to allow the audience to like her.

The Flawed Body

Our bodies make an enormous impact on the kind of person we become. Whether we are smart, strong, fast, awkward, blind, weak-hearted, beautiful, easily addicted, or posses poor balance, our bodies shape who we are. That's just the nature of things.

This must also be true for the hero of our tale. She must have some physical condition that affects how she approaches the world. A strong, stupid football player will have her struggles, just as the highly intelligent, confined-to-a-wheelchair will have her own.

Something about the character's physical self holds her back. It could be permanent or temporary, such as an injured foot. It is a physical flaw.

The physical flaw is important, because it sets a crucial symbolism to take place during the story; the spiritual triumph over the body. More on that later.

The main character, or any character for that matter, must possess a response to the world that is due in part to the limitations of her body. A main character's responses could be slightly different from the responses of typical people in the world, but those responses must include a combination of the influences the world has imposed, and her physical traits.

Put aside any thinking you may already have about your character's mental state, and describe what she looks like, what physical limitations exist. There should be some flaw in her body, which would have applied pressure on her development.

It doesn't have to be a physical handicap, it could be something in the brain, such as no sense of rhythm, or no smarts. For the purposes of character creation, how the brain functions is part of the physical body. Whatever it is, it should encumber their achieving what they desire.

Some examples of body flaws and affects on a character; a scrawny child might have developed using her brain and good people skills, to avoid trouble with bullies. Someone not too bright might lift weights to compensate for seeming dumb, a limitation such as height might cause a person to stoop, or to wear high heels.

Be careful not to allow a harsh world and body to have beaten down your character. There should be hope for improvement. Your character might be a thoroughly bitter and unhappy individual, but keep in mind that everything and everyone must have value.

Talent

Just as the world we've created has a value, so too must the character we create. We will call this a talent. The talent could mean being good at something. It could also represent a positive quality, maybe the character slows her car down for squirrels crossing the road.

The hero's talent should attempt to compensate for the existence of flaws, both in the world and in herself.

What is that something of value your character possesses? There must be something she is good at, or something she believes is important. A sliver of pride in an otherwise cruel life.

This is a complex and important part of our character and her creation. This is also important for the audience The audience must find a reason to like our character early in the story.

The audience must quickly identify with that talent, that something of quality in the main character, so they can root for her, can care about her, and identify with her. It should be something endearing. Even a small positive characteristic can accomplish this while showing the need for improvement.

Figure out the body flaw, and talent, and add those to your growing list of sentences.

The Desired

There are things in life we all want. Perhaps a reader of this book desires to tell a good story. Perhaps a mother wants her child to grow up safely. At times, desire can take over our lives. Historical accounts reveal how people have lost kingdoms in pursuit of desire.

This chapter will cover a character's desire. It will offer an example of how her desire can connect with a world flaw to demonstrate the character's flaw. It will end with a brief discussion about desire lost.

A character's desire is the primary vehicle by which the external plot and internal problem intertwine. The internal problem is evidenced through the character attempting (and failing) to acquire something she desires against the backdrop of the external plot.

Whatever that thing is that is desired, its existence in the story serves three purposes. It will give the audience someway to hope for the character to succeed; it gives the hero a way to become an active participant in the story; lastly, it offers an opportunity for spiritual growth, as the character must overcome the power desire holds over the spirit. At some point she must give up achieving what she desires.

The power desire holds over our lives can be debilitating. Humans can desire something so bad that we throw away other things that should be important to us. Unchecked, desire can grow to become more important than even life, and reason. A character's spiritual development needs to incorporate ways to overcome desire without rejecting that which is desired.

The hero doesn't have to desire something shallow, such as the newest dishwasher. (That could be a good choice for showing a materialistic person.) Desiring peace, or love, can show a quality many of us value, while leaving the character exposed to heartbreak and disappointment. Desire also acts as a story mechanic to show the conflict the character has about the world flaw, establishing that in her heart she is unhappy.

Imagine a story where the world's problems is that kids have no outlet for their energy. Because the kids have no outlet for their energy they take to spray painting. Now let's suppose there is an angry old man who get's upset at about that spray painting. He feels resentful toward the kids and chases them away. His approach might be flawed.

By showing the man with his desire for a clean neighborhood, the story changes the character from a mean jerk into a person who cares about his world. The internal problem and the external plot can now exist together because his desire presents an understandable, if flawed response.

The world flaw is that kids have no outlet. The character's response is to chase the kids away, which reinforces this world flaw. But his desire to have a clean neighborhood does not address the real flaws of the world. He is responding to the symptom of that world flaw.

This shows how the flaws of the world have shaped the flaws of the character and that his desire is perpetuated, and he can not find happiness.

All conflict originates inside the hero, and reveal the flaws present within the character and the world. The character is conflicted. The character wants to respond to the threat against what is desired. The character isn't able to overcome the idea that such flawed responses are part of the problem.

The audience will begin to figure out what could be done differently, and thus discover the flaw. The character's initial response to the problems of the world must work against achieving what is desired.

The conflicts that exists in the world are really conflicts within the character. The internal problem drives the external plot.

What the hero desires will remain illusive until she has overcome the problems of the spirit. The great irony is that to overcome the problems of the spirit means the hero will have to abandon the quest for what she desires. Desire must be abandoned.

Introduction of what is desired happens during the stage Normalcy (see outline below). What is desired is not accessible, at the minimum it is not fully accessible. Failure to have desire fulfilled must be present at the beginning of the story.

Try to use different methods to demonstrate how the hero feels about what is desired. She might draw pictures of the desired, or sing songs. Consider creating a ritual used to approach that which is desired, or to approach anything else in the story, for that matter.

A side note on a desired lost:

If the character starts off in possession of that which is desired, and then loses it, such as through the death of a loved one, the story becomes one dealing with loss. For matters of character development, loss is backstory. A story dealing with loss is a story about healing, which has its place. Healing is about getting better, not about a spiritual transformation.

For a story dealing with loss to become a story about spiritual transformation, the character must have already gone through a healing process, and come to a mental state where a new desire can exists.

Character Flaw

It is time to get to the character's flaw. This chapter will cover laying out the character's internal problem in sentence form. Unfortunately, this book cannot tell you what the character's flaw is. Think about the various story elements you have already created: the world, its flaws and values; the world danger; the character's physical form; her talent; her desire. All of these should be pointing to a simple flaw.

A flaw that is simple works best, because the story is about overcoming a flaw, not how cumbersome a flaw can be. A flaw is a response to something flawed in the world. When explaining the character flaw, break it into two sentences. The first is the HOW sentence. How do you show the flaw? You will eventually write many pages of this in your story. For now, try to keep it to a concise description.

The second is the WHY sentence. The Why asks for a description of what is going on inside the character. This is something you may never state for the audience. Still, you should understand why a character responds the way she does. This should be a simple problem that can be overcome within one story.

For an example, let's return to the movie <u>Nemo</u>.

A father fish named Marlin tries to control everything that happens to his son, Nemo. That is the How.

The Why is, to Marlin, the world is a dangerous place, and he has promised himself he will never let anything happen to his son. Marlin's flaw is that he assumes he can control Nemo, and that doing so will keep Nemo safe. Try writing similar sentences for a character you might want to use in a story.

Look over what you have written down so far. You should have a world with a flaw, a joy, and a world danger. You should have the typical responses by the general population, a main character with a physical flaw, a talent and a desire. You should now write down the How and Why of the hero's internal flaw.

Take this list of sentences you have created. Set them aside, and allow them to percolate while you read the rest of this book. Look back at your list and see if you can create a story using those sentences along with the other ideas presented in this book.

The Rule Of Three
or
The Threat of a Pattern
or
1, 2, Three Ends Different

Many students of writing will roll their eyes at this chapter. It's importance may have misstated, been overly stressed, or openly mocked as an old fashion crutch for storytelling. Be careful of dismissing the rule of three too quickly. There is a subconscious reason for the rule of three to exist.

For those who are unfamiliar with the rule of three, it is the idea that any good story or joke must have three parts, and that those three parts can be broken down into three smaller parts of three.

The Rule of Three can be effective for channelling the attention of your audience. This is true for one very simple reason. People are wary of patterns.

A pattern is a repetition of the same thing four times in a row. Patterns represent that which is expected, and does not change. If it does not change, there can be no growth. It is stagnant. It is bad for the character. It is bad for the audience.

Human's are keenly adapt at spotting and avoiding patterns that are harmful. Drought, animal attacks, flooding. Patterns are to be avoided. The Rule of Three taps into this subconscious avoidance during storytelling. It demands that change will take place after two repetitions. 1, 2, three ends different.

Think of the story, <u>Goldilocks and the Three Bears</u>. In this story, a girl named Goldilocks is lost in a forest. She finds a cottage in the woods and goes inside. There she finds some bowls of porridge set upon a table. She is hungry and tastes the first bowl of porridge.

The first bowl of porridge is too hot, she goes to the second bowl of porridge and finds it is too cold. She tries the last bowl and finds the porridge is just right.

If the story had gone on to tell how the third bowl of porridge is too salty, and there is a forth bowl of porridge, the story is ruined. It becomes a list of all the ways porridge can go wrong. It risks becoming a pattern. The third bowl must be 'just right'. 1, 2, three ends different.

<u>Goldilocks and the Three Bears</u> expands the rule of three into a total of three such experiences in this home. After she eats the porridge she finds some chairs. One is too soft, another too hard, the last is 'just right'. Again the rule of three.

At last she moves to the bedroom with three different beds, one too soft, one too hard, the last is 'just right'. She falls asleep.

Here it would seem this story has broken the rule of three, and repeated the three different experiences three times and had the same three results; the last ending is always 'just right', three times in a row. However, when she falls asleep the story does change.

A group of bears enter the house. The story reveals that the house belongs to these bears, and they are not happy that their house is a mess. They finally locate the intruder, and eat her. Well, maybe the story has her running away, or something. I can't remember.

The point is that after the third experience the story changes. Something happens to prevent there being a forth of anything.

Other stories that use this rule is <u>The Three Little Pigs,</u> and <u>Three Billy Goats Gruff</u>.

There is a universal understanding among humans, which attract us to stories that present change. To do so there must first be an established threat of a pattern.

Nothing signifies spiritual stagnation like falling into a pattern of failure. Patterns are fine if they produce crops and healthy offspring. A pattern that harms people is to be avoided.

The Rule of Three speaks directly to our capacity to identify danger. Dangerous patterns in nature must be dealt with quickly. This is why people develop prejudices and suspicions. People want to identify and stop a threat, before it becomes a pattern.

A great example of this exists in the axiom, 'Fool me once, shame on you. Fool me twice, shame on me.' The unspoken part of this axiom is that the third time the foolery is attempted, things are going to end very differently.

A last example is a knock-knock joke instead of a story.

Knock-knock

Who's there?

Banana.

Banana Who?

Knock-knock.

Who's there?

Banana.

Banana Who?

Knock-knock.

(usually the victim sighs here) Who's there?

Orange.

Orange who?

Orange you glad I didn't say banana?

1, 2, three ends different.

If the 'Banana' response had been repeated one more time the listener of the joke probably would have walked away. Try it out sometime and see what happens.

The rule of three is versatile and useful in so many aspects of writing. Not just because it is good practice, but because audiences are subconsciously tuned to looking for patterns to be broken.

The hero should face failures in groups of three. Successes should be presented in threes as well. Keep this rule in mind as you read forward.

Audiences need to experience stories in a multiple of ways. For stories to be meaningful we must be use such subtleties. The Rule of Three should be present in many aspects of your story. Still, break some things up to avoid creating a pattern of threes. It's tricky, I know.

The Catalysts and Symbology

Earlier was discussed how a character will refuse to change. She will even refuse to accept the need for change. Due the character's resistance, the story will need some things to get the character to start moving toward change. These catalysts are sometimes called the calls to action. A later chapter will discuss the Three Calls to Action.

The story will incorporate two external catalysts, and one internal catalyst. These catalysts are; the object, the guide, and the self. The object catalyst is something that presents an incongruity in the world. It could be a magical sword that must be wielded by a spiritually advanced person. Perhaps it is something small, like a lucky penny. It could be much larger, such as an alien spacecraft. Whatever its size, it must be something that doesn't fit with the way the character understands the world.

The guide catalyst is a person who will encourage the hero to take an action that will challenge her sense of self. The guide must, by all accounts, appear to be a better person than the hero. Perhaps the guide is not perfect, however the actions of the guide must be superior, in ways that provide the hero an opportunity to reflect upon how she responds to the world. This offers a contrast of behaviors that push against the hero's complacency.

Together, the object and the guide expressly layout for the audience how the character needs to change. Despite this, the character will still refuse to change.

Having the object and the guide come from outside the character's world allows for an elevated sense of spiritual change. It suggests that some things exist beyond the confines of basic humanity. It hints of the ethereal, of the angelic, of Godliness.

The object and guide don't have to be supernatural, or even magical. These could originate from a different culture, or a different state. They could come from a different school or church. By having them come from outside the character's world the symbolism suggests power, and knowledge, that exists beyond our common understanding.

The third call to action must originate from within the hero. Only the hero can decide to change, for change to have any really meaning.

Much could be said about the affects that rules and dogma have on confining spiritual development. Suffice it to say, when a person challenges themselves to spiritual advancement, what they are really doing is challenging the rules and definitions established throughout life, or that have been set up for them by a community (parental rules, peer pressure, places of worship, etc.). Only after letting go of rules and dogma, can a person find spiritual growth becomes accessible. The character must be shown abandoning the of her rules of world. Only then can she create new rules, test those rule and find success as a process.

The catalysts help her on this path, but cannot be shown doing this for her. This is why she must refuse the calls to action that originate from outside of her own desires. The last call must originate from within herself.

The Object Catalyst

There is a greater discussion to be had about the Object Catalyst. The object catalyst is, like it sounds, an objet that attempts to get the character to take an action. Using an object catalyst in your story has a profound reason for existing in a story.

Even though this first call to action will be refused, the very presence of an object at this point in the story represents great symbolism. There is a permanent affect upon the hero that takes place at the discovery of the object, which cannot be accomplished with any other storytelling tool. A psychological examination of the impacts objects have over us in our daily lives might reveal this connection more clearly.

Human beings use tools in ways that are unlike any other species on Earth. When humans experience an object during our daily lives, it is part of our nature to consider how that object can be used as a tool. We can't help it.

The idea of turning an object into a tool has important significance in our minds. Tools represent survival, advancement, and prestige. With a tool we can build shelters to survive the elements. A tool can shape our mental, personal, and spiritual awareness. A tool can express cultural norms.

At some point in our childhood, most of us have found a stick on the ground, and used it to poke at something we are unsure of. In doing so, we have created a tool.

Many might recall taking the time to break off smaller twigs, and pull away loose bark, to fashion the stick in a way that suits our idea of the purpose it should serve.

In doing so, we each have imbued in our tool some changes which represent the way we think the tool should appear, and how it should work. We've put a little bit of ourselves into that tool. It could be said, the tool, the stick, then becomes an extension of our ideas, of our culture, of ourselves.

The next person to use the stick-tool would be instantly aware of the changes made to the stick. They would see where we've broken off some twigs, left others. This person may be in awe of the work we've already done.

On a subconscious level this next person to use this stick might then see the world a little bit differently, a little bit more as we see it. When they use the tool, a subtle difference will take place in how the or she might hold the stick, and in how the world might be viewed.

Understanding this is important to understanding the object catalyst. Let's discuss a different tool to explain further. Let's consider the hammer.

Nearly everyone has swung a hammer to hit a nail. Most of us have the three-dollar hammer laying around the house. You grab this hammer, hold the nail and try not to hit your thumb.

Tap-Tap-Tap-Tap-Tap. Tap-Tap. Tap. Simple. However, not all hammers are built the same.

Suppose you try a different hammer. Suppose you try a hammer created by someone with expertise, and new ideas about how a hammer should function. When you pick up this well made hammer something subtle, but important, takes place.

If you started with a three-dollar hammer, and switched to a thirty-dollar hammer, you will notice stark differences between the two. The better hammer is balanced much differently. The grip is changed.

You will have to alter the way you hold the hammer, the way you swing it, the way you hold and hit the nail. Repeated use of this improved hammer will allow you to discover that you don't need to tap the nail over and over. Two or three good hits will finish the job, quickly. It will require practice, and learning new skills. This too will shape how you approach life.

Using a good hammer can change the way you view the world. That's a bold statement. But it is true.

You will develop new respect for carpenters and roofers. Using a good hammer can generate new ideas about how things are put together, and how to complete tasks. A good hammer may alter the quality and workmanship of the things you buy, which might shape how you arrange the furniture in your house. The effects of using a good hammer can cascade throughout your life, and change the way you consider nearly everything. You may never be aware of it happening.

Other things can have a similar affect on us. Think how your life is different with a faster computer (can you ever go back to a slow computer?). Consider how you feel after driving a well made car. Using a fine musical instrument. Can you imagine trying to live life without your cell phone? All of these tools affect how we experience life and what we expect will happen. Each one changes how we view the world. Each changes what is possible for our future.

When we use a new tool, one that is well made and fashioned by someone else, we assimilate ideas that to us are revolutionary. We internalize new thoughts on how the world can work. How it should work. Our actions are changed as a result, altering many other ways we live life.

There are subtle suggestions present in every tool about how to approach life. While not directly, or even consciously, an audience can understand that these subtle suggestions exist. We are each altered subliminally when we experience an object that is both new and well made.

In a way, you could say, the tool has manipulated us. The subject and object are reversed. The object becomes the instigator of change that takes place within us, the subject. We pickup a hammer and it controls us, forcing us to see the world in a new way.

Do you start to get the idea about the power of the object catalyst? This subconscious connection an audience has with tools creates a powerful symbolic message to exist in stories that use an object catalyst as a spark toward spiritual transformation.

Of corse, the hero will reject the object catalyst, but it matters little. The mere existence of the object has the subconscious permission of the audience to begin a process of change in the character. It is a change which will become fulfilled throughout the rest of the story.

Because the subconscious understanding of the audience accepts that a tool can shape our world view, they will also allow for the spectacular to exist within this object-catalyst. The symbolism of change that the object represents is so strong that the object can be of fantastic origins. It can hold magical powers, in an otherwise nonmagical world. That is the power of the object.

Again, in any story, the audience will be asked to suspend belief, accept the extraordinary as possible. The introduction of the spectacular elements are best focused at key points, and the introduction of the object catalyst is such a point. It has a spiritual reason for existing, because the audience innately accepts that there is a power in tools which can instigate change. Thus, it is possible to make this object extraordinary.

However, there are some requirements to impose on the object catalyst for it to hold a powerful place in the story. First the object catalyst has to be something made by someone other than the hero. Preferably it should come from outside the character's world.

If the character knows the person who gives this object to them, you may need to make this person the guide, or someone very important to the main character. It could be someone who is no-longer part of their lives, such as when the object is left behind in a will.

The object might come from another planet, or a magical creature. Keep in mind that this object cannot be from the small world your character inhabits. This is important because it must hold ideas that are new to the hero, free of the world flaws and character flaws that already exist.

Three Calls To Action

or

Catalysts and Cataclysms

At the beginning of the story the character is flawed, and doesn't see a reason to do anything differently. She doesn't want to change. The three calls to action provide the momentum to get the character changing. As stated earlier, these are the Object, the Guide, and the Self.

The first two calls to action must actively be refused by the character. The hero is complacent in her flawed life. She has settled in to her habits, and is at risk of turning into a pattern. Only after refusing the calls to action will she come to realize, on her own, that she must begin her journey toward spiritual transformation.

The three calls to action must be presented in differing ways. The first call would ideally arise from an object. The second call should preferably come from a guide. The third call must spring from the character's own need to solve a problem.

When the character is first called to act it should be subtle. Obfuscation in the first call to action will allow the character to ignore this call in a way that is believable. The refusal to act here is not a high level of resistance.

Aligned with the first call to action, is the growth or appearance of the cataclysm (see chapters below). The cataclysm doesn't have to be anything grand, such as an Earth shattering asteroid, but it might be. When the character experiences the first call to action, the world must begin a process of undergoing a change, which will prevent the character from returning to her previous life (more on this in later chapters).

The second call to action occurs with the arrival of a guide. This is a person that will show our character what path she should aspire toward. The presence of the guide should be problematic for our character, for a couple of reasons.

The guide is just so darn good at everything, his or her very presence is an indirect call to action. Perhaps, depending on the story, the guide will directly make a call to action. Such as, "Help me defeat the bad guys!"

The guide might have the respect and admiration of other characters. The call to action from the guide will be more difficult to refuse than the first call. The hero might resist with the phrase, "No way. I like my life how it is."

The last and third call to action preferably comes from within the main character. She is compelled, by the conflux of the external plot and the internal problem, to accept change. The hero might seek out the object or return to the guide during this stage, seeking help to resolve an external plot point. The story arch will have the hero making the choice to decide to act, and ultimately deciding to accept spiritual change.

In the beginning of an ideal story, the character is living her life without thought. She attempts her daily pursuits of the desired with minimal success. She is in a state of complacency.

When the first call to action is presented with the object, the character has no desire to do anything different. She will ignore this call to action, or even respond with a conflicted-response.

At this point, the demonstrations of her failure must grow more obvious. This is when the guide appears, and the second call to action is given. Change is undesirable for our character, so this call will be shunned.

The character must face a greater failure, have near misses with the world-danger, and stronger problems from the external plot. The hero will come to understand she is unhappy. She will realize that she needs to act in order to get what she thinks she wants. She becomes her own call to action. She will most likely return to the object at the point, and be unable to fully access its potential, or she will return to the object near the end of the story, as a way to demonstrate her complete transformation.

The more active the hero's role in accepting the third call to act the better it will show the character choosing to change.

The character must initiate her spiritual transformation. No one can make you change, except for you.

This completes this section of the book. The next section of this book covers the stages of the character development.

Story Outline: The Beginning

For reasons of practicality, I am breaking the story outline into three parts, beginning, middle, end. Each part consists of a series of stages. A stage is a key event taking place in the story that can help demonstrate how the character is progressing through her development. The stages aid the storyteller in establishing the character's different ways of thinking throughout the story.

When considering how to apply the stages below, keep in mind that these are not plot points. The plot of your story will need to be added on top of the stages mentioned below. While it is possible to combine stages and plot points, the purpose of the stages are about character development. One might wish to have chapters alternate between plot and the stages presented below. Ideally, the plot will work with these stages seamlessly.

Beginning:

Normalcy

First Call to Action

First Call Refused

Introduction of the Cataclysm

Normal No More

Normalcy

The story begins with the character in her daily life. Everything seems normal. She is living a life that is normal for the character and the world, before the external plot begins.

The events taking place in the stage Normalcy can be as mundane as school kids sneaking behind the gym during lunch, or it can be as exciting as hunting deer in the monarch's forest. It could be killing zombies.

This is a period to introduce the audience to the main character and world using action. It is important to establish the character's physical traits, and hint at the internal flaws and talents. It is best if you can also introduce what she desires.

That's a lot of information to present in the first moments of a story. Accomplishing all of this makes this introduction to your story a very active one, and it forces your audience to pay attention. They like that.

The stage Normalcy will most often show that the character is content. The hero believes life is good, that she is in touch with herself and is happy to pursue what she desires. This stage will also need to present a hint of the character's internal flaw. When the the internal flaw shows itself, the world danger will also make an appearance. The hero avoids the world danger, and the first hints of the internal problem emerge to close the stage.

The exact definitions of the internal problem should remain

shrouded to the audience, unless it is a short story, at which point you've got to get things moving. Usually, the weight of the internal problem has to grow over time. The storyteller must start off knowing the internal problem, the audience has to discover it.

Introducing the talent and desire early gives the audience a reason to stay with the character, until they learn enough about the character's internal problem to fully identify with her, and then they will want follow the story through to its conclusion.

During this stage, the audience needs to learn the rules of the world, and come to understand that not everything is perfect. The stage of normalcy will provide the groundwork for spiritual growth to occur, which will encourage the audience to stay with the story.

First Call to Action

In the stage normalcy, the character is fine with her small failures. So, something must introduce the character to the idea that a change is required. Preferably, an object.

Something about this object must actively suggest a need for change. This can be done through writing attached to the object, it could be an overt invitation to engage with the external plot. It could be an artifact of great importance that is revealed to the character. It could be something simple yet unique, such as a toothbrush from the future, or a penny once owned by a famous person.

While this object does relate to the external plot, it will call upon the character to act in a way that challenges her established routine of life and her flaw(s). When the external plot asks the character to break away from Normalcy, it is also asking her to break away from her internal complacency, to break away from her flaw. Because this internal shift is difficult, the character will not be willing accept the challenge.

She will refuse to act. There is an internal story-reason for the character to refuse to act. She does not want to change.

It would be ideal if the object has some level of connection to the flaw, or with another stage in the story. Maybe this connection isn't revealed until later in the story. It is more important to have an object than to have a great connection, as will be explained in the next chapter.

First Call Refused

After the first call to action is made, the character must decline that call to action. While this is an extremely brief event in the story, this stage is given its own heading here to point out how important it is that this takes place. The hero doesn't want to change. The hero must put away the object catalyst. She could walk away from it or she might put it in a drawer.

This is an active choice to ignore the ideas represented by the object. The point is, the character must attempt to get back to life as normal.

The act of refusing or putting away the object catalyst is important, because it draws a line separating the power of the object and the eventual change in the hero's personal struggle. If the refusal is not marked clearly there is a possibility for the audience to believe that the object has caused the change in the character, placing the character in a passive position. For spiritual transformation to occur, the character will have to decide to change on her own, not be compelled to act, even if only by appearances.

The earlier discussion about the power of an object to alter our thinking demonstrates why the eventual change taking place in the character must be shown as an active choice, as much as possible. Without having a clear mark that the object has been put aside, or its call has been denied, any change in the character could be attributed to that object, instead of to internal spiritual growth.

The object might encourage the hero to change, but it should not be the reason the character chooses to change.

Spoiler alert: The following example points to such an error in the movie, <u>The Hobbit</u>, <u>An Unexpected Journey</u>.

At one point during this movie, the character Bilbo has been unhappy about joining the Dwarves on their trek, and he is considering returning home. He then becomes separated from the group, where he comes across a golden ring.

He puts on the ring - a powerful object from outside his world - and the act of wearing the ring is given great notice through imagery of the ring seeming to slip onto his finger magically. We witness that the ring gives him great powers, which he uses to escape the creature Gollum, and to become reunited with his group of travelers.

Bilbo, still wearing this ring, overhears a debate about Bilbo's questionable participation. He suddenly appears amidst this group, exclaiming that he has decided to stay with the group, and will help the dwarves on their journey.

The audience has to assume that bilbo removed the ring in- order to appear, and we are shown him slipping something, probably the ring, into his pocket. However, Bilbo's use of this incredibly important object happens nearly simultaneously to his decision to aid the dwarves.

The personal journey of Bilbo as an active character is destroyed. The story is completely ruined.

It is quite reasonable for the audience to wonder if perhaps there is residual power of the ring operating inside of this Hobbit. Perhaps it is the ring which has caused the change in this character's decision to stay with the dwarves, and not the character himself. The possibility of Bilbo experiencing a spiritual transformation is completely lost.

Because of this one scene, The Hobbit becomes hollow backstory for the rest of the series. The audience is left wondering if it is the ring or the Hobbit controlling fate. The entire theme over the series of movies is destroyed as well, as we must now wonder if it is the work of individuals that shape the world, or if it is the whims of mindless evil stored in the metal of a ring that controls all of fate.

It is with this example that all writers must be cautious to place important events in well defined stages. Keep the story- reason clear about why things happen when they happen.

The object catalyst must be refused, or at least be put away in a separate scene (hopefully followed by more failure).

Otherwise, the object poisons the character's active role in the story. At the minimum, the object should be put away, and the character expresses a distaste for the object.

It may be that the story should portray the character somewhat enamored of the object. This is fine to reveal through a brief expression. But this should quickly be masked by an outward statement of distrust or distaste. The character can be moved by the object, but she must return to her denial of it, soon thereafter.

Introduction of the Cataclysm

Once the first call to action occurs and is refused, cracks in the main character's contentment become apparent. This is the time to introduce an approaching end of the character's world. A deadline should appear, which represents the changes the character must go through; this is the reason why a cataclysm exists.

A cataclysm sounds like something that will affect the whole world. It could be a war, or a disease. It doesn't have to be so destructive. Keep in mind, the use of the word *World* encompasses only the immediate world of our character. When your world takes place around a house, something as simple as moving to a new neighborhood is a cataclysmic event.

The cataclysm represents an end to the old self, and the beginning of the new self. It also represents that there is no turning back once the changes have begun. A third symbolism exists with a cataclysm, it represents the hero's fear about her impending spiritual transformation. Change is scary.

The cataclysm must start small, perhaps only as a suggestion. It will grow in intensity through the rest of the story. Due to its heavy symbolic nature (symbolically representing the destruction of the old self), there is leeway available to create an extraordinary cataclysm. The audience will be willing to suspend belief, and will accept that the cataclysm can contain remarkable events in an otherwise non-remarkable world. This is the time to add elements that expand the depth of the world. Lastly, try to avoid a ticking bomb as a cataclysm. The need to have a hero race against a clock of time, such as on a bomb, can add excitement. And in a pinch for a plot, this can be acceptable. However, try to find a cataclysm that is more directly tied to her world and it's flaws. This will enhance the emotional connection, and urgency, for the audience.

Normal No More

After the main character has refused the first call to action, and has been introduced to the cataclysm, she must seek to return to life as normal. The character needs to continue to peruse what is desired. However, the old life is no longer accessible.

Any attempt to achieve the desired will fail more dramatically. The world danger should press harder. The presence of the cataclysm will grow more intense. The audience will better understand that the need to change is growing. Tension is raised.

There is no more normalcy. Change is coming. The hero, having rejected the first call to action, learning of the cataclysm, pursued by the world-danger and failing to get the desired, just begins to realize her old life is slipping away. And, she does not like it.

Story Outline: The Middle

These stages show the character being forced to deal with the growing need for change.

Introduction of the Guide

Second Call to Action

Second Refusal

Cataclysm Approaches

Cataclysm Not Avoided

Expand The World

Conflict with the Guide

Proof of Need for Change

The Hero Apart

Third Call to Action

*Revelation

  The Unsure Self

  The Three Quiet Resolutions

    Awareness of Self

    Resolution with the Guide

    World-Joy

  The Hero Perfected

* Includes a subsection of The Unsure Self, the Three Quiet Resolutions, and the Hero Perfected.

Introduction of the guide

A guide arrives. The guide is a person, though it could be a computer or something that has an active role. When I use the term Guide, I am not talking about a guru in robes, or the mage with a beard. It could be, but sometimes the goodhearted, best-friend-all-along can become a guide. The guide could have been in the story earlier, but the role as guide needs to be applied at this point, at least in the mind of the storyteller. It often helps to have the guide be from far away.

Whomever your guide turns out to be, she will seek to engage with the main character over a matter relating to the external plot, perhaps the cataclysm. The main character will not understand the guide's point of view. The two will disagree over something, either about how to react to a plot point, or perhaps something more direct.

It becomes clear that the guide does everything better than the hero. The guide seems happier, might even have some level of access to the thing that is desired, which the hero is lacking, depending on what the desired is. It is possible to have the guide making mistakes right along with the main character. In this case, it is the guide's reactions to these mistakes that sets the guide apart from the main character.

The guide is the better person. The main character secretly knows this, but she won't accept it. All the better if the guide comes across as a little bit bumbling. Consider giving the guide her or his own flaws and desires, as well create a body flaw for the guide that is in opposition to the hero's. Tensions should grow between the guide and the hero.

Second Call To Action

Something about the existence of the guide will serve as a call to action. It might be that the guide makes a direct request to act, to help solve the external plot. Not all stories allow for such direct communication.

The second call to action could be something subtle, such as how the behavior of the guide could imply the need for the main character to undergo an internal change. It could be a direct challenge by the guide.

The hero and the guide should discuss the oncoming cataclysm. This ties the message of the guide to the character's refusal to act, despite the mounting destruction facing the world.

The existence of the guide is a threat to the hero's complacency. Even if the hero respects and adores the guide, there should be some subtle grumblings about the guide taking place within the hero.

Even though the guide could be a best friend, the guide should from another world. This is not a hard-fast rule, but it is preferred. Remember how I define world; it doesn't have to be another planet or a different country, it could be the family next door that does things in a very different way. The guide must possess thinking that is foreign to the main character.

Second Call Refused

Symbolically speaking, the guide represents the state-of- mind that the main character will eventually strive for. The differences that exist between the hero and the guide offer the excuse on which the hero can refuse to change. Subtle or direct, the second call to action must actively be refused by the main character. The decision to change must come from within, and should not happen at the suggestion of another character.

The guide's call to action could be direct, a request to fight monsters. It could be indirect, such as, when the guide reveals an emotion about an experience that runs in contrast to the hero's stated position. Such things depend on your story. To the hero, the call to action must strike the hero as odd. "I would never do that."

After this refusal to act, the hero faces greater failures in the plot. The hero's conflicted-responses must grow more intense. The world danger causes more problems. The cataclysm becomes more powerful and unavoidable.

Some stories might use the refusal in a more subtle manner. It is possible for the hero to attempt to fulfill the second call to act, but be unsuccessful. This is a passive method of character development, as the hero acquiesces to the request for action, but just fails because she has not yet made a transformation. Yes, it is still shown with her taking actions, but the lack of her refusal is not tied to her failures.

The Cataclysm Approaches

Along with the second refusal to act, the problems for the character intensify. So too must the urgency of the cataclysm. The external plot will get more complex, too. The story can become multidimensional at this time, which can be useful in giving the characters something to work for, or against. A distance should grow between the hero and what she desires.

The world is threatening to break apart. The hero just wants her old life back. Things have started changing and there isn't anything to stop it. The hero will get pushed to the point where she will have to acknowledge that some action must be taken to avoid the cataclysm.

These tensions, along with the presence of the world danger, and the compounding pressures to change, will grow to a crescendo. Everything is falling apart, the desired is unaccessible, the dangers of the world are hounding her. Something has to give!

Expand The World

At some point during the story the hero should have her world expanded. It is a great idea to include the hero traveling to a new location. It could be visiting a different school, or going on a job interview. It could be an adventurer traveling to a far away mountain.

By expanding the world, the obvious metaphor is created of the hero on a journey. We also show the hero expanding her experiences, and expanding her mind.

The hero will come to see that no matter how important her personal problems might seem, the hero is just a small part of a much larger universe.

This unspoken introspection in your story speaks to the audience's understanding of spiritual growth, which must include the realization that the drama and problems in our own world are small, compared to the great complexities of life. This introspection shouldn't have to be overt. Allowing your hero to take notice of new scenery can be enough to suggest a readiness to expand toward a spiritual transformation.

The placement of this stage is not so set in stone, it is more important that travel take place. Let this stage serve as a reminder about the importance of travel, and how that can demonstrate the change the hero must undergo. It makes sense to place travel after the introduction of the guide, and after the second refusal to act.

Cataclysm Not Avoided

The cataclysm intensifies the internal problem, and the external plot. The hero might actively attempt to stop the cataclysm from taking place, in the easiest possible way. The act of trying to avoid the cataclysm reminds us of the wish to return to the earlier contentment.

This is a wish that cannot be fulfilled. Of course it fails. Contentment is not achieved. This stage is short lived, and minor, but it is included here to keep in mind the power the cataclysm has in the story. The cataclysm must grow in relevance to the character's struggles against change. It is here to show her growing desperation.

Conflict with the Guide

The growing cataclysm conveys the growing stress within the main character. Her failures, and the world danger, are unavoidable. As a defensive mechanism the main character will find something else, or someone else, to blame.

When we humans are confronted with a failure in ourselves, many of us look to divert responsibility toward others. We all might have done this at some point in our lives, such as a child trying to get away with taking a cookie, and claiming the dog ate it.

This tendency to avoid responsibility, by redirecting blame, gives the character a realistic reason to avoid recognizing he or she is causing all the problems. It is realistic that the hero avoids dealing with the real cause of the failures, by blaming the guide for those failures.

The guide has access to what is desired. The guide appears to be really great at everything the character is secretly wishing she could do. In the mind of the hero, it must be the guide's fault.

If the hero is a mother who wants a close-knit family, the guide will have access to the troubled teen who is rejecting that mother. If the hero wants a loving pet, the guide can get the dog to do tricks where the hero was unable.

The main character comes to resent the guide for her own inability to access that which is desired. The hero will transfer inner disappointment onto the guide. Jealousy might drive her to even attack the guide.

At some point the guide must leave. It could be that the hero pushes the guide away. Perhaps the guide has as an errand to run, maybe the guide just dies. Whatever the method, the main character must find herself on her own, and experience the third call to action.

Proof of Need for Change

Once the guide has left, the hero will attempt a task on her own.

This may be an attempt to return to the life she once knew. It could be that she goes after what she desires. It might be the hero tries to mimic the guide.

Because she is not enlightened, she will be unable to really do what the guide does, and her actions come off as desperation. This failure may even push the desired farther away. It is this failure that really introduces the hero to the idea that she doesn't really understand anything.

This is the proof of the need for change. It is not the third call to action yet. It does establish how the third call to action will unfold. There is no guide, or anyone else, to blame. The hero will have to accept that she is responsible for her failures.

The Hero Apart

After the proof of need for change, the main character retreats. She moves away from the other characters. The hero wonders why the failures are getting worse. She considers that she may be what is the problem. This poses the question, how is this shown?

To answer this we must first ask, how do real people change the way they think? It isn't enough to decide that something different needs to take place. As stated, smokers decide to quit daily, yet they still light up. What is it that happens to allows people to really change?

Understanding this profound question is an important part of a great story. How does a real person change, and how can a story show a person changing?

When it comes to real people, there are many types of behavior that can be altered. If people were to walk around with their eyes closed, without looking where they are going, they are apt to trip and hurt a knee. The pain in our knee will set new thought processes in the brain, which will help us remember to be more vigilant when next we go walking about. But, what about thought processes that do not produce physical pain? How do we change the negative ways we act and react when we do not have physical pain to guide our decisions?

Decisions to change behavior take place at brain levels that cannot be not swayed by rational thought. The processes that control deeply rooted behavior won't be compelled by promises, or placations for improvement. On the contrary, the human brain is prone to create false rationalizations in response to poor outcomes that are derived from poor choices.

For example, a jilted lover might seek companionship in strangers, and he may feel a temporary sense of righteousness or validation from such interactions. However, when all the strangers have left, more feelings of emptiness follow. The brain may not be able to understand these emotions are created from empty experiences, that they are the result of the actions taken to combat the initial feeling of being jilted.

Instead the brain sees these new feeling of emptiness as a new sensation, and a new event which needs to be remedied. The previous remedy of seeking out temporary companionship provided a relief before, so the behavior is repeated, with similar results, and perhaps additional personal drama. A cycle of bad behavior has been created.

Something is needed to break this flawed way of thinking and acting. For the brain to change such behaviors, it must respond to a certain type of pain. But, we can't hurt the brain the same way we hurt a knee. Instead, a different kind of pain must be used to inform the brain on how best to behave.

Emotions are used to communicate with the brain. Different and painful emotions will affect how the brain responds, if done correctly.

When a person recognizes that he or she has made a social faux pas, that person might experience embarrassment. If someone has hurt another person accidentally he or she may experience a sense of being mortified. These are forms of pain that occur in the brain, and can alter how the brain responds in the future.

This kind of pain can alter behavior. This is the way to communicate with the more instinct-driven parts of the brain. Emotional pain can establish that serious changes in the patterns of thinking must take place. Emotional pain can be a life changing event. But, when it happens, it can happen in a quiet moment of reflection.

Emotional pain is a very personal experience. It takes place in a way that is void of words. So, how do we show such changes happening inside the head of a fictional character?

We are lucky that most people can witness this taking place in others. Witnessing this often takes place at a subconscious level, yet we can understand the impact and implications when we see it happening in others.

It might be enough to show the hero in a pensive moment, or expressing an emotion of embarrassment. Think of the actions your body would take if you felt a certain emotion. Your eyes might get wide, you might cover your mouth with your hands. Perhaps your eyes would well with tears.

Attempt to present this stage with few words. As long as certain points are touched on, a story can present the idea of this emotional change taking place within your character.

This is, in essence, the beginning of the spiritual transformation we are awaiting. It is merely a recognition that the current state of thinking is flawed, that different behaviors should be applied.

Avoid a prolonged sense of self blame. Soon as the hero recognizes she is the problem, the choice to change happens quickly. This is the setup for the third call to action.

The Third Call To Act

From out of the stage Hero Apart will spring the third call to action. It is a swift transition but needs its own heading as a stage. It is at this point the character decides to make the change. She realizes her actions have been pushing the desired away. This is the third call to action, and it originates inside of her.

We humans are not defined by what we think, but instead by what we do. Our brains are not prone to thoughts unless those thoughts are solidified through action. True spiritual change can only be achieved by demonstrating control over our thinking and our actions, and over that which has power over us: desire, the world, the body. All must be taken on and defeated.

By no means should you consider the character to now be in a better place, mentally. The character might feel contrite, but this doesn't mean they won't continue to make mistakes. She may instead go too far in a different direction to make amends, or to show they want to try. This stage must be followed by the Three Failures.

Yes, she has decided to be better. But deciding to change doesn't change anything. Real change takes a lot of work.

Revelation

The stage Revelation is an over arching stage. A super heading that exists over a number of chapters: The Unsure Self, The Three Quiet Resolutions (broken into 3 more subsections), and The Hero Perfected. Revelation is a process where the hero learns who she wishes to become. This is a blended transition between the middle of the story and the end of the story.

It is rooted in a confrontation between the hero and the guide (or the conflict between the hero and the ideas represented by the guide). This shows the hero attempting and being unsuccessful at spiritual change. Her attempts end in failure. She is still resistant to change. In essence the hero has to give up *trying* to act different, and just be different.

Throughout the following sections one, or more, of several things need occur:

1. She comes to understand there is always more to learn. She can never be perfect. This is a moment where the hero admits he or she doesn't know what to do. None of us know what to do, so the audience can relate with her.
2. The hero will realize there are matters more important than her selfish desires.
3. The hero comes to understand that other characters, (such as the guide) are capable of feeling hurt, and that hurting other

people is not a path to happiness.

4. The hero accepts that to survive requires working with other people, such as the guide. Accepting help is a good thing. No can succeed alone.

There are steps in this stage where you have freedom to apply humor in an otherwise non-comical story. Humor is important to show character growth. Humor happens when we are able to step away from ourselves, and we can laugh at our mistakes. This feeds on our ability to look at a situation from the perspective of a third person. It may be difficult to expressly have the hero laugh at her foolishness, but it is perfectly useful to have the audience laugh.

By allowing the audience to laugh at the failed attempts of the hero they will subconsciously relate to the character, and will fully realize the flaw and how silly it is, and that it needs to change. As well, the audience will be all the more drawn in when she finally does achieve spiritual transformation.

To have something revealed means, until that moment, something could not be understood. We start with a hero who realized she is lost and confused.

The Unsure Self

The hero's actions define who she is. When she seeks to change her actions, she in in essence deciding to alter who she is, what kind of person she is. Her self identity is cast into doubt. The examined life is never an easy one.

The central focus of this stage is to show the hero entering into a mental state that is not solid. She wants to abandon the flawed parts of her personality. However, nothing exists to replace those. She will try out different things, but doing so is akin to guessing at an answer, and not knowing the answer. As a result the hero's thinking and actions can be portrayed as irrational. This is a time for action, emotion, and perhaps even humor.

There are qualities of insanity present in the character's state of mind, and these should be evidenced by her actions. The hero rejects the old self, and is flailing about wildly trying to be someone else, maybe trying to be someone she is not. She still doesn't get what it means to experience a spiritual transformation.

The hero must make attempts to create a better self, which end with failure. These attempts can be shown in whatever order, or method, works for your story. Here are some options.

1. The hero adopts mannerisms of the guide. These attempts will be over exaggerations, which could be humorous, or very sad.

This is the character trying to replace herself with something she admires, admitting the importance of the guide in the hero's life. Disaster ensues.

2. The hero confronts the desired, with questions such as, 'Why do I even try? Why do I even care?' Of course the hero cares. At this realization the hero may fall into a brief moment of despondency, followed by a brief fit of rage.

3. The hero may do something dangerous or drastic, it could be a confrontation with the oncoming cataclysm (which is now very strong). It could be an attempt to give in to negative aspects of people she cares about, and failing because this isn't who she wants to be.

4. The character could confront her flaws, by confronting the world danger. Because she is not yet in control of her transformation she will be unsuccessful and meet a very large failure.

Keep in mind the mental state of the hero. The hero is struggling to be something new, and does not know how do it. Desperate and exhausted, the hero will collapse. Nothing is left except her new desire to be something besides who she has ever been. The truth about life is revealed.

Do her actions stem from a real sense of self? More likely she acts in ways that mimic what she thinks others will find appealing. Is life a fumbling attempt toward an imagined self? These nihilist questions are left unspoken, but the audience understands the implication of them.

It is from these ideas that the audience can empathize with the desperation of the hero's desire to be re-made. She admits the need for a transformation, but she is unable. She must be fully broke, and lost before she can gather the strength and determination to continue, for what else is left except her wish to be something better. Only from complete destruction can something new be established.

We now need to take the story and slow it down, so that it can be digested and understood, and believed, by the audience.

This is what the next few sections aim to do.

The Three Quiet Resolutions

The three quiet resolutions break the previous intensity, and action, of the story. All the energy from the confrontation, and resistance the character has had, is channeled into overcoming the internal problem.

The three quiet resolutions are:

Awareness of Self

Resolution (with the Guide)

World-Joy

Awareness of Self

If one searches the multitude of web pages on the topic of free will, many ideas abound about what that means. Wise people contemplate the process of decision making trying to understand free will. Some scientists use instruments and scans to observe the electrical activity of the brain to explore thought process taking place.

There is strong evidence to suggest that decisions take place in the brain before an individual is aware a choice has been made. A person might feel as though he or she is mulling over a complex set of reasons for or against an important decision, but we aren't. The decision takes place in the brain before a person finally comes to accept that decision.

What is believed to happen during these moments? Generally, our brains respond to requests for decisions through electrochemical reactions between neurons. There may be two, or more, chains of possible reactions to a choice taking place simultaneously; different neural connections race toward completing a thought simultaneously.

One of those competing neural connections will 'complete' first, and this will rigger a response before the others. Decision paths that are completed more frequently stay healthy, whereas paths that do not result in actions may atrophy. The ability of those neurons to complete successfully in the future is depleted. This allows patterns to exist in our behavior. It is sometimes called a learned response. These learned responses are solidified in the brain when an action is applied to those thoughts.

When the completion of certain neural synapses take place our "decision" is made. Only then will our conscious mind 'be informed' about what decision has been made by the neural connections. Only then will our conscious mind understand and accept the decision, and put such decisions into words.

This allows us the sensation that our conscious self has made the choice, when really any sense of deciding (the feeling that 'we have made a choice') is a secondary response to brain activity already having taken place. We think we made a choice only when the brain has told us the decision. Is there a difference? Yes. The actual decision took place much earlier than our awareness of that decision, as it relates to how fast the brain works.

This suggests something about how decisions are made. We believe we are actively deciding what happens. In truth we are mostly unaware of what choices go into our daily lives.

It is only after neural connections have completed are we able say to ourselves, 'that is my choice'. It is after we are pushed by our brains to act that we come to believe we have decided. Our self definition is formed by our actions, not by our conscious thoughts. Ideas of who we are exist as thoughtful reflection of the examples of our past actions that we can point at to better understand who we are.

If we wish to be a different person, how can we change well established behaviors? We cannot simply desire to be unaffected by a decision making process over which we have no control. We change our behaviors by refusing our initial responses, and taking an action - any action - that runs contrary to the initial inclinations to act. It is through actions that we can alter how our brain functions.

Only when a smoker decides finally to go against the well established neural connections that cause one to light a cigarette, will a new neural path be created. In the great argument about free-will, these rare moments of establishing new behaviors are what this author would consider to be free-will.

In the same way, the stage Awareness of the Self seeks to present the hero moving the decision making process beyond giving into her learned responses. This stage is an expansion from the moment of self doubt, discussed in the Hero Apart, and hints at an ability to make choices with a greater purpose 'in mind', rather than succumb to her first responses.

This is what the stage Awareness of the Self confirms in the story. It is a statement that the character will no longer be controlled by past habits, and ways of past thinking. It is a moment to alter her self, beyond what past experiences have encouraged the character to do.

Specifics about how this is done is left up to the storyteller. As one of the quiet moments it should be brief. The hero will stop herself from taking an action that had previously been part of her accustomed habits. She will take an action that is new, or in contrast to previous behaviors.

Rely on the early part of the story to setup such a change in decision, which can now be shown again and replaced with a different reaction. The act of making this choice cannot be stated. There is no tell that can work in this moment. It must be the act of carrying out an action that's contrary to the previously established inclinations and actions.

True Morality

Morality is a fascinating topic. Great volumes have be dedicated to the idea of morality. Religious passages will attribute, and base, morality on the works of scribes. These are false moralities. True morality can only stem from within a self that is void of external influences.

True morality is free from edicts and dogma of organized religion and law. Both religion and law are corruptible. True morality remains a constant.

A religion might mandate the stoning of suspected adulterers, but the real immorality of applying a death sentence in these cases is clear to other cultures. How can morality exist as two separate constants?

The law might allow sentencing a murderer to death, but the very contradiction of killing someone for murder only affirms that the morality upon which this law is based has been corrupted by a desire for control. It draws from a desire for revenge, and can act as a mask for political maneuvering, and thus it is not moral.

Awareness of a true morality by the individual requires a very personal understanding of right and wrong. One is either moral or not. There is no bible or legislative directive that can apply true morality into the heart of any individual. True morality must come from within, and only great people, only true heroes, can know true morality.

Because true morality exists free from edicts and dogma, there is no room for a character who must learn morality. The hero cannot be shown learning about morality. As important as being in touch with morality is to a character's spiritual transformation, there can be no words, no passages, nor stages present in this book to convey to the audience that true morality is understood by the hero.

The hero simply must be shown to understand true morality. She must be at her core a person of virtue. Her spiritual transformation will be powerful enough. Her actions will show she is a moral person. This is that one thing that sets her transformation apart from the object catalyst. It sets her transformation apart from the call to action by the guide.

This makes her transformation a thing that is hers. This is the stage that does not exist, for a reason. By never being suggested, true morality becomes proof that she is now touch with her inner-self, and that her inner self is at its most base point a good and moral self. She is now an equal with the guide. Perhaps even better.

Resolution with the Guide

After the actions of the stage, Awareness of Self, the character now shows she can apply this new ability to change her behaviors, and interactions with other people. The hero shows she can work with the guide as equals.

The hero no longer feels threatened. The hero's self identity is based on an openness to be part of life, and not to fight against it. As this is another quiet resolution, this can be accomplished with a smile, a handshake, or hug. It can be both the hero and the guide (or someone else) taking on a simple task together, or taking on a bigger task such as defending against the cataclysm, or possibly escaping the world danger, or some unexpected trial.

Any more than this and the resolution with the guide can become a distraction. Keep it as a brief demonstration; the character has changed. For the purpose of a story, this can be an acknowledgement with the guide as above, or to someone who can suitably fill in for the guide, if required.

These quiet resolutions could be placed into one scene or setting. The will probably work better to be spread out. Certainly, the stage World-Joy will have more power when presented on its own.

World-Joy

The world-joy is a pleasure the character has not experienced until now. Perhaps the hero has never seen it, or has seen it but cannot access it. This unknown pleasure must have been displayed very early in the story. If the character has never experienced it, then the audience needs to see other characters experiencing it. The audience must be primed to identify with this world-joy. It is a symbol of spiritual transformation.

Show the world joy as a rare and fleeting experience. The symbolism is that the character could not participate in the true beauty of life until she was willing to experience change.

The world-joy will become available to the character after she has taken steps to improve her spiritual self. It might come even later in the story, after the external plot has been solved, toward the story's final resolution. However, it can be a wonderful token of change and success to offer to the audience at this point, before the final struggle to resolve all the conflicts of the external plot have taken place.

The discovery of the world-joy is the symbol of inner contentment with the changes the character has undergone. It is a quiet, personal joy. Because the world-joy is rare and fleeting, the time spent experiencing the world-joy need take only a few moments. A simple hint at the pleasure of the world-joy is enough to represent the satisfaction and happiness that comes with spiritual growth.

Examples of world-joy; a sunrise, music, a good meal, a rare flower, catching fish. Whatever the world-joy is, remember that it must be something unavailable to your protagonist until after they've changed. The world-joy must be accessible to other people in your story before this point. The world-joy can't be that everyone can now catch a fish.

I have reservations about using a first kiss between characters as the world-joy. This tactic has too strong of a tie with someone else to count as a world joy. If there is a love interest in the story, the first kiss may come at the reunion, later in the story, it might also come at the sacrifice.

The world-joy is something to be experienced alone, as an example of spiritual contentedness. Sharing the joy with another character breaks away from solving the internal problem, and steps into the realm of external plot. World joy is about personal accomplishment.

While this is a quiet resolution, and an internal experience, it does not have to be quiet at all. It is a moment where the character finds the world joy on their own.

This could take place in a noisy crowd. It could be hitting a baseball out of the park. One of my favorite examples is in the movie, School of Rock, where Jack Black's character had tried to stage-dive early in the film, and been unable. Only after his transformation, and after his sacrifice, was he able to achieve the stage dive and attain the world joy.

The Hero Perfected

The stage, Hero Perfected acts as a super heading for the end of the book. Yet, at this point the external plot will show the hero working toward a goal using the new actions and thinkings she has discovered. She must show she is in tune with her true morality. The hero is demonstrating that her behaviors surpass previous actions. It need not take long.

The importance of this is very strong. She must affirm in the mind of the audience that she is different.

The End Of the Story

The character has appeared to have made a spiritual transformation. Now it is time to put that transformation to the test. At the end of the story the hero proves herself.

It may be useful to think of this as the Section of Mastery. The hero must show she is now in control of the things that were problematic earlier: desire, world danger, body. All must be mastered.

Journey of the Improved Self
Sacrifice
    Decision To Sacrifice
    The Sacrifice
    The Cataclysm Strikes
Aftermath
    The Hero Alone
    The Hero Reflects
    An Active Life
Rebirth
    Putting the Object to Use
    World Danger Tamed
    Overcoming the Body
Salvation
Final Resolution

Journey of the Improved Self

The journey of the improved self never really ends. It isn't a moment of, 'I made it' and, "Now I can settle down and be happy ever more". The journey of the improved self is about accepting that growth is ongoing. It takes continued effort throughout life to be the best person possible. A favorite quote I've heard states, 'Today I will do a little better.'

All journeys have a beginning. For us humans, ours begins with birth, or at least our teenage years. For the main character, her spiritual journey begins at the end of the story. Until now, the character has been resisting change. Deciding to change is not the same as changing how one approaches life.

The end of the story displays new approaches to life through several events. Each will challenge the character to prove change has been made. These will reaffirm her spiritual transformation has been complete. The character will have to overcome the initial elements established at the beginning of the story.

There are trials and successes the audience will need to witnesses, to fully understand the character has transitioned into a state of mind that will remain into the future. I call this The Journey of the Improved Self. Each step has smaller steps, and these all present the character as one who has broken free of the worldly ties, and instead is more interested in being the best person she can be.

The main parts of this section are: Sacrifice, Aftermath, Rebirth.

The sacrifice will take require some build up, including the decision to sacrifice. Then the actual sacrifice must be experienced, which happens nearly simultaneously as the striking of the cataclysm.

The aftermath will slow the pace of your story down, to allow the character to find herself alone, to reflect and make clear to the audience that she is content with the choices that have been made. and that she can now have an active life.

This leads directly into Rebirth, Putting the object to use, Taming the world danger, and overcoming the limitations of her body.

From here the hero will find salvation, and then the story's final resolution will follow, and should only take as much time as is absolutely needed. This is the last part of your writing, and you never want your audience thinking, 'When will this story end?'

Sacrifice

The sacrifice takes place with the actual arrival of the cataclysm. The hero comes face to face with the risk of oblivion. She also understands that with the cataclysm comes a risk to what is desired. The hero is compelled to sacrifice her own needs (or herself) to save that which is desired, even if it means losing the thing that is desired.

By sacrifice I mean, the hero gives something up. It could be her own safety. Perhaps it is her life that is at stake. Another important thing to keep in mind is, she is also giving up her pursuit of that which is desired.

A sacrifice must have meaning in the plot, so the sacrifice should be a story related act of honor and courage. It should abandon all fear, and only exist to save others, or save the desired. This is a process where the old character dies in a figurative sense.

Perhaps the hero does actually die. What is most important is that this death is symbolic of the death of the old self. It represents a death of the flawed way of thinking.

If your story has covered the previous stages correctly, the audience should understand how important that which is desired has been to the hero. During the sacrifice the hero gives up obtaining the desired. By doing so she demonstrates her ability to see and respond to the world in a way that is improved.

The audience is saddened by the hero losing what is desired, as the audience has hoped for the hero to succeed. However, the audience is also enamored at the courage shown to take the higher road, to work for the better of others. A demonstration of morality.

It happens quickly. There are three sub-stages that best represent the sacrifice. Some of these seem like no brainers, but are presented to be sure you show the audience that these things take place. Be aware of them as you write, and your story will be more powerful. The three parts are; the Decision to Sacrifice, the Actual Sacrifice, and the Cataclysm Strikes.

Decision to Sacrifice

For the spirit to be free and accepting of change, all the things that inhibit the spirit must be overcome. The first one to be given up is the power desire has over the spirit.

The hero's spiritual view of the desired shifts, to the point where the safety of that which is desired becomes more important than the hero having access to it. The hero's desire has transformed into unconditional love. The hero wants the best for the thing that is desired. She has control over her responses to ensure that what is desired is protected in the face of the impending cataclysm.

Removing the power desire has over the spirit is different from shunning desire. Shunning things that are desirable is not acceptance. If monks shun contact with something desirable they have not exhibited self control.

It is better for the hero if she wants the best for things she holds dear. To want the best for what is desired removes the power desire has over the spirit. It allows for the loss of access to what is desired to offer a sense of fulfillment, because what is desired is at last in a place that is safe.

When the hero can appreciate that the desired is in a better place, she has found the source for true happiness; love. Love is giving. Inner peace comes when we are able to overcome our obsessions with possessions, and instead celebrate the possibilities of selflessness.

The Sacrifice

Having decided to carry out the sacrifice, the character shows she has the conviction to follow through in the face of danger. It shows determination. The main character must then make the sacrifice. It can be moving for the audience to indicate a realization of the sacrifice, through the eyes of someone else.

Determination and bravery. This is what is going on inside the mind of the hero. Those characters who observe the sacrifice will have much more complex emotions about what is going on.

These emotions do not need to be explained. Your audience is quite capable of imagining these for themselves. Show someone gasping at the sacrifice and it will carry a powerful meaning.

The choice to sacrifice is very important. It is the active desire of the hero to alter her initial responses. While one can find forgiveness for actions of self-preservation, by choosing to sacrifice the hero demonstrates in the most direct way her free-will to be something better. It is proof of self control, and self determination.

Cataclysm Strikes

Once the spiritual confinement of desire has been realized, and once the decision to sacrifice has been made, it is time for the forces of the external plot to meld with the internal problem in a climactic moment. The cataclysm strikes. The hero is sacrificed.

The impending doom that affects everyone sets in. Examples of sacrifice at the cataclysm; a flood where the hero saves the desired, but is washed away; one employee must be fired and the hero resigns so that others may keep their job.

This is a climactic moment with lots of action and reaction. It works well if everyone, including the audience, believes the hero has actually died.

Aftermath

The Aftermath is what happens to the character after the cataclysm strikes, and after the sacrifice. These are the moments where the story slows down again. The following fulfill this stage: The Hero Alone, Realization, Active Life.

The Hero Alone

The hero alone is different from the hero apart. After the cataclysm the hero is cut off from in a world transformed. With no access to the desired, or to others who are familiar, the hero should take refuge in a secluded place, a room, a cave or tunnel, some place hidden.

This secluded spot symbolically shows the hero retreating into her mind to gather her thoughts. While it might seem like a setting, this is a stage based upon its symbolic power and must be shown in clearly defined terms.

Realization

Taking in the devastation, the hero will come to understand the life they had known is now gone. What they desired is lost, their old self is no longer accessible.

The spiritual transformation is well underway, yet the full demonstration of this is not complete. The hero has just overcome the power of desire, but must still master the world and the body. The hero must be alone to gather thoughts and prepare. But, just for a moment. Adding a moment of sentimentality here might also work for your story. Perhaps, show fond remembrance of what is desired, along with peaceful acceptance that the desired is safe.

An Active Life

Now is the time to avoid a new complacency. It is a moment to venture out into the post-cataclysm world, and to discover what new work can be completed. This shows the hero actively embracing change. The hero might build a shelter or aid some animal in distress, but the hero probably won't have time to complete a very large task. The hero is about to get interrupted.

Rebirth

Personal Call To Action

Much of the story is resolved. There are a few more important parts to wrap up. To do so we need to get the character moving toward a new goal. This is the purpose of rebirth.

Rebirth begins from the growing confidence of the character. The next step in the story is prompted by a Personal Call to Action. This is the symbolic proof that the character has made a true transformation, and will act against future, or past, spiritual stagnation.

This is best shown as wrapping up a previous plot point, a closure to something about the cataclysm, or exposing and resolving an element of side story, or backstory.

Self motivation here speaks of self reliance, and strength of the individual. A more solid and active character is shown when the hero is responsible for this stage. She starts putting together a world she wishes to see, wishes to live in. It isn't so much about her rebirth, as it is more about rebirth of the world.

The world is the hero's to recreate, which goes hand in hand with rebirth. The world is reborn along with the character. The hero sees the world has changed, and so the world will be made anew.

It could be the discovery of a new land. It could be the building of a village, or uniting people into a new community. How it is shown will depend on the plot of the story.

Putting the Object To Use

As an extension of the mentioned Active Life, the hero should apply the wisdom of the object. The hero has moved past her initial rejection of the object, and has come to terms with the message it offers. The object can now be controlled and used to the benefit of the hero, and perhaps others.

It isn't crucial that the object be used at this point. It could have been used a little earlier, such as during the sacrifice, or perhaps a little later. However, it is desirable that the full abilities of the object be exercised at this stage to demonstrate full competence, and a complete control over the character's understanding of the transformation having taken place.

It is also a great time to put the object to full use as it can be a sign to the world danger that the hero is in control.

The World Tamed

The cataclysm has struck and things have calmed down. Yet, the world is not powerless to cause harm. The world is very much a threat. Flaws in thinking can arise as a result. The potential for fear is a constant. The world danger will be thrust at the main character one last time.

Recall, this danger should have been present in the story much earlier, hopefully from the beginning. The symbology of the reappearance of the world danger shows the world will still have its flaws, still have things to be afraid of. The character must stand firm and not give in to new dangers or new fears.

The hero must take on the threat of the world danger and tame it, but not destroy it.

Mastery of the world danger is not destruction. It is not defeating the world danger or being better than it. The world danger is not the main villain who will die in a last attempt to trick the hero. Overcoming the world danger is learning to control the impact fear has on our lives.

Here the character will see the world danger with new eyes. The hero's world view is changed. Spiritual transformation is more powerful than fear.

The world danger could be a wild beast that is tamed. It could be the bully that becomes a best friend. It could be the boss who offers the hero a promotion. Something dangerous about the world is turned around, to work with the hero, and not against the hero.

This represents an end to being effected by things beyond our control. Spiritual growth remains solid in the face of fear. It shows control over fear and a willingness to befriend things once misunderstood.

Taming the world danger should be an active stage in which the danger is reintroduced after the cataclysm, and the character responds differently, and develops a friendship with what had once been a threat. When the hero uses the object in front of the world danger the object can be a tool to unite the two.

Sometimes, just the strength derived from a spiritual transformation can affect self confidence to the point where it can instill newfound respect in the world danger. Having gone through a spiritual transformation, the character can now generate a new respect from others in a way that is realistic. This will also allow the world danger to befriend the hero.

That is, when a person is comfortable with the changes he or she has undergone, it can create an awareness in others of the positive thinking taking place in the character. People notice and respect others who are confident.

Not just people, but animals will notice strength. The taming of the world danger shows the transformation has occurred and is visible by the world. When the world danger becomes aware of the changes present in the hero, even if not overtly, it sets the stage for collaboration and unity. The world danger now has a different response to the character as a result. The danger now wants to befriend the hero, and will not attack.

Overcoming the Body

The limitations established by the body flaw are no longer powerful enough to shape the character. The hero will overcome her body flaw, and in essence correct that flaw, showing such limitations exist only in the mind. Real life may not always work this way. An amputee may never recover a lost limb. However, she might learn to walk with a prothetic.

The audience longs to believe that miracles really do happen. The extraordinary can happen during this stage, but some limits of reality should be applied to prevent the story from becoming hokey.

Ways to show overcoming the body could be the child with a broken foot takes off the cast. It could be the dumb jock uses his head to solve a problem. Perhaps the weak-but-smart girl finds physical strength to move an obstacle blocking her path.

In the movie Forrest Gump, Forrest as a boy who has crippled legs learns to run, his leg braces fall away as he is no longer defined by his seemingly frail body. The power the body had over the spirit is defeated.

Once the final limitations of the body are defeated, the hero can take on the challenge of resolving some issue in the external plot, and succeed. It is a success in the external plot as a result of the successes in the internal plot. Internal success leads to external success. An outward statement of achievement.

This stage is a fine one to place as a final confrontation with any antagonists, or to begin wrapping up confrontations in the external plot. What happens in the story and how it relates is where the skills of storytelling take place. Keep in mind that this stage can be dramatic, and fill the audience with exhilaration, if it occurs with overcoming some obstacle in the external plot.

Salvation

Salvation is the hero safe, and returned from the exile that occurred during the Sacrifice, or the major confrontation. It is the return of the victor.

The hero receives recognition of her success. Salvation shows a level of acceptance by people of enlightenment, that the hero is now one of them. It could be demonstrated as a reuniting with the desired. It could be cheers from an adoring crowd. It could be congratulations from the guide. It all depends upon your external plot how this is shown.

I suppose it would be possible, for a story without a positive ending, to have the sense of salvation originate from the audience and not from the story; that moment when it becomes clear the hero loses the external plot but has achieved a lonely success on the internal problem. Hamlet comes to mind.

Salvation is important in the story as it shows veneration, a personal reward, not for the accomplishment of the external plot, but because of the internal changes that have occurred and the successes that have arisen as a result.

Final Resolution

The point of the final resolution in a story is not just to wrap it up, so the audience can go on to the next story. There is purpose to the resolution that serves the message of spiritual transformation. It should only take as much time as is absolutely needed.

Still, there are three parts here that can be displayed in rapid succession. These parts should show the character from somewhat of a distance, in a new setting, now accepting of change, happy in the new world.

The character uses new skills along with the world danger, now tamed, at her side. Optimally, the desired is shown safe, and perhaps working with the main character as well. Both facing changes and challenges without fear. It is key to show the continued success over the world, desire and body.

As the last step in this book, I will now construct a story using the tools outlined above. Following that will be a discussion of the stages shown in that story.

Story: Vandalism

Joe Gothbury opened the front door of his row house to a spring morning to get the morning paper. The covered bus stop in front of his house caught his eye. Someone had sprayed on a four letter word for male genitalia.

He'd hated that bus stop since they'd put it in seven years earlier. He'd gone to city hall when Transportation installed the thing. They'd treated him like an idiot. Now it was an eyesore.

The stop was dark brown, right in front of his home, almost part of his house. It was the first thing he saw every morning. Now it was covered with spray paint. Again.

"That's it. I've had enough!" Joe stepped all the way out onto his stoop to look up and down the street. The sidewalks were empty. The street was was lined with parked cars. A single yellow taxi glided by. The park across the street was empty. The playground's brick wall was six feet tall, sprayed with the similar words. All the play equipment was broken, and trash scattered across the patchy grass and weeds, pushed by a light breeze.

Joe snatched up the paper, and twisted his arthritic knee. Aches had been almost constant recently. He shuffled back into his house, and closed the door.

Tabitha took the steps down from the second floor, traveling the little path she'd made in the dust. The cat stopped near the bottom and meowed once up at Joe.

"Good morning to you, too," Joe growled.

His slippers hissed against the worn, hardwood floors of the hall as he shuffled to the kitchen. Joe set down the paper and picked up the phone. He mashed the number for the department of parks and services, responsible for vandalism of city property. "Hello. Parks and Services." a man's voice said over the receiver.

"I need to report a vandalism," Joe said. "Is this you, Mr. Gothbury?"

"Yes. This time it's the bus stop right in front of my house. It's been spray painted. Again." "The bus stop?"

"Yes. The one that's right—"

"I'm sorry, sir, but we can't handle bus stop vandalism any more. You need to call transportation."

"I need to call transportation? Unbelievable." Joe rolled his eyes.

"Yes, sir."

"I need to?"

"Well, sir. You know the details and—"

"You guys are just trying to get out of doing any work!" Joe kicked the table leg, exasperating his arthritis. "I pay my taxes. And for what? There's been more and more vandalism recently, and you guys don't do anything about it."

"We are very busy, sir. And orders from up top are that we need to divert resources to more important matters. We can't stop for every bit of vandalism that takes place in the city. If there has been damage to your property you can try the police department."

"That's all you got?"

"I'm sorry, sir. We can't do any more at this time, the budget is getting cut and - -"

"Forget it!" Joe snarled, and slammed down the phone.

Tabitha curled around his legs, purring and meowing. Joe ignored her, took a breath and grumbled, "I need my coffee."

He went to the coffee pot and poured a cup-a-black and went to the dining room, which he'd turned into the TV room. He eased back into his comfy-chair.

Joe set down his coffee and tossed his hands in the air. "Ah! I left my paper in the kitchen. I'm so angry I can't think straight."

Tabitha meowed at the kitchen door, pushing against the door jamb, turning and rubbing again.

"All right. I'll feed you." Joe pushed himself out of his chair and shuffled back to the kitchen where he dumped too much cat-mix into a white bowl, set on the floor next to the half-sized fridge. Loose cat food scattered over the floor, joining the mess around the refrigerator. The cat purred again, rubbing against his legs.

"There's your food. Eat. Dumb cat."

He ignored her continued rubs and purrs.

"I'm going to have to do something about those spray painters myself."

He did his best to stalk to his room, located behind the kitchen. His knee ached so bad, it mostly came off as limping.

A small lamp lit the sparsely furnished room from the nightstand.

The room had been a utility room he'd turned into a bedroom. Dingy wall paper peeled at the upper corners, where dust-webs hung in clumps and strands.

He changed into his beige trousers. He pulled on black socks and thick-soled black shoes the pediatrist had said would help his feet stop hurting. He pulled a blue windbreaker on, and a red-white-and-blue baseball hat with a logo for hotdogs, he got free from some promotion. He reached behind the wooden bedroom door and took the old golf putter he kept there in case of an intruder.

"It's a matter of personal responsibility," he said. "People need to take care of the things they have in this world. If the city won't stop the vandalism, someone has to do something."

Tabitha worked at his legs, rubbing and purring.

"What's wrong with you today?" Joe gave the cat a small shove with his foot.

She glared at him and ran out of the room. The sound of her angry howls and running up the stairs echoed through the empty house.

Joe rolled his eyes and shook his head. He made his way to the front door. He set his jaw and pulled open the door.

The bus stop was no longer dingy brown and spotted with grey cuss words. It was spray painted with white and yellow. A spray paint can rolled on the sidewalk, as if just dropped.

A person wearing a dark-blue jacket walked away from the bus stop. The hoodie was pulled up over the person's head.

"Hey!" Joe called out.

The person didn't turn around.

"Hey! Stop!" Joe felt his neck stiffen with anger. The person started running.

Joe waved his golf club in the air and started down the stairs.

His knee made a popping sound. Pain pierced his right leg and he cried out. He leaned against the wall at the bottom of the stair, panting, waiting for the pain to subside.

After the pain faded he pulled himself off the wall and looked around. The hooded person had gone. The spray paint can caught his eye.

Careful of his knee, he bent and picked it up. The can had fresh yellow paint oozing out the nozzle. It had a weight that felt good. He gave it a shake and it rattled. The nozzle melded with the tip of his finger so perfectly.

He pointed it at nothing and pressed. It made a hiss noise and a fog of yellow sprayed out. Feeling guilty he looked around and tucked it under his arm.

Limping up the front stair, he went into the house and staggered down the hall. Tabitha meowed at him from the top stair. Ignoring her, he went to the kitchen. Garbage spilled over the trashcan. He set the spray paint can on the counter next to the trashcan.

He pulled down the arthritis medicine, popped a pill, and dropped into a metal-framed chair next to the round, formica table. The newspaper lay on the table. The headline told about tax cuts being voted on in the general assembly. Below that was an article about budget cuts, and a picture of the mayor smiling his famous smile for reporters. The city was cutting funding to police, parks and transportation.

"I still pay too much, for what? No good services, that's what. They're all incompetent."

Below was an article about various parks around the city to be torn down. The park across the street from his house was slated for destruction. Demolition would begin today.

An old memory stirred, of him on sitting on a bench by that playground on a warm afternoon.

"Well, at least that's one less eyesore we'll have to deal with."

Shaking off the mood, he went to the fridge and pulled out a package of cream-filled chocolate cookies. There were only two left.

"Gah! I have to go to the store."

He stepped outside and limped down the front stairs. The painted bus stop was so bright and cheerful in the otherwise dreary street. Despite patches of empty space in the painting, there was attention to detail in subtle ways, transforming the bus stop into a thing of near beauty. "Who gave them the right?"

He limped past it.

An older couple was dressed in well-pressed clothes, waiting on the steps of a neighbors' home. They held flowers and some sort of covered food dish. The door opened, and a woman who lives there gave them hugs and invited them inside.

Passing the park, he noted the swings hung in disarray. The merry-go-round was off its axis.

He went inside the store on the corner. It sold beer, smokes, candy, bread and sandwich meats. The air inside was cool, the lights fluorescent.

Sami, the store owner greeted him from behind the counter, "Good morning."

Joe had tried to ignore him for years, but the guy never stopped greeting him. Joe grumbled something he thought could be taken as a politeness. He found his package of cookies and put it on the counter along with a five.

"Did you hear about them closing the park?" Sami's accent was almost a song. "They're tearing it down today."

"Yeah. Good riddance to that mess." Joe tapped the five on the counter: Tap-tap-tap.

"No. Not good riddance. We need that park." Sami picked up the five and started counting change.

Joe said, "That place is broken and falling apart. We need that like we need a road full of holes."

"Ah. We need our roads to be maintained, just like our park." Sami dropped the change into Joe's hand, pulled a plastic bag from behind the counter and started fiddling with the edges, to open it up.

"Nah. Those kids don't care about anything," Joe said. "They'll just destroy it again, and then my tax dollars are wasted. That money is better used in my own pocket."

Sami got the bag open and put the cream-stuffed cookies into the bag. "The park is broken because kids think we don't care about them." He handed the bag to Joe.

"Well, we don't. Not if they can't show any respect for what they've got." Joe turned and walked toward the door.

"For five years I've been selling you cookies. This is the longest conversation we've ever had."

"What's your point?" Joe stopped and looked over his shoulder.

"When is the last time you had a conversation with one of those kids?"

"Bah!" Joe pushed out the door, onto the sidewalk. "Have a good day," Sami called out, as always.

Joe limped back up the street. City workers had shown up at the park, wearing orange vests and hardhats.

The kid in the blue jacket was back by the bus stop doing something to it. Joe got closer and realized the person was spray painting. He marveled at the daring. In broad daylight, with the do-nothing city guys able to see it all. If they cared enough to turn around.

Joe formed a plan. Staying quiet, he eased up behind the painter. He got as close as he could and grabbed the neck of the person's jacket.

The hood pulled down. A girl with blond hair screamed and twisted around. "Let me go."

"No, you don't! You're going to pay for all those bad words you're putting up."

"I don't write bad words. I cover 'em up." She hit his arm and pulled away.

Joe's grip broke its hold, and he tottered off balance. He brought his right leg forward to catch himself, but it 'popped' again. He cried out in pain and fell over, his bag of cookies sliding away.

"Oh, my God. Are you Okay?" The young woman put her hands out.

The pain in Joe's leg was excruciating, he shoved his fist into his mouth.

"Don't die on me, old man. I'm sorry."

Joe clenched his jaw, "I'm not going to die. It's my leg." "You want me to call an ambulance?" she asked.

"No. Just, help me up." He waved his arm for her to take his hand.

She pulled him up and backed away. She stooped and gathered his grocery bag with the cookies, and handed it to him. "Are you all right?" she asked.

The pain in his leg was blistering. His forehead beaded with sweat, and his vision swirled. He tried going up the stairs. It took all his strength to tackle the first one.

"You sure I shouldn't call an ambulance?" she asked.

"I don't need your help." He leaned on the brick wall and took the next step. *Seven more to go.* He paused to take a breath, panting.

The girl came up behind him, lifted his arm and wrapped it around her shoulder.

"What are you doing?" he asked.

"Helping. Isn't that what neighbors do for each other?"

She was strong, looked to be about 20. Something about her face tugged at old memories. She grabbed his waist and helped him up the next step, and the next.

"I'm Joe." He bit back the pain.

"SB," she said. "But, you can call me Susan."

At the top of the stairs they paused. He leaned against the wall and panted, feeling confused.

"I know you," Susan said. "You used to sit in the park and watch kids play. There was a pretty woman with you. What happened to her?"

"She died." Joe fumbled for the key in his pocket. "I'm really sorry," Susan said.

He pointed at the bus stop. "You're one of those kids that defaces everything."

Susan gave a slow shake of her head. "My stuff isn't that bad, is it?"

He looked at the painting. The yellow and white were filled with bold streaks of red that blurred through the layers from the top right, as if the sunrise were breaking through. A rough dragon with green and red scales occupied the space that had been left earlier.

Something in its expression possessed intelligence with a hint of sadness.

"No. It's actually pretty good," Joe said, "but it's still vandalism. Go paint your stuff for an art gallery. Don't deface a public bus stop."

"I tried the galleries, but they're filled with snooty know-it- alls, full of their rules of what counts as good. I gave that up. Now I try to make the world better by painting over cuss words. You know what I find? Those words don't show up on top of my art. I think whoever is doing it is just angry."

"Angry? Angry at what?" Joe asked.

"At how horrible this neighborhood has gotten. It just needs someone to look out for it. That's what I'm doing."

"It's not your place to look out for the world." Joe pointed his finger at her.

"Then who's gonna look out for the world if not me? The city isn't doing anything to make this world a nicer place. It's like no one wants to spend money or do anything. We all know it. The kids do too. That's why they're painting those bad words."

"Then they should get a job and stop painting things that don't belong to them. Did you see that park? They've destroyed it."

"No one destroyed that park." She pursed her lips into a grimace. "Things got broken, and no one fixed them. Why are *you* so angry?"

"I'm not angry," Joe said. "All right, I am angry. That used to be a great park, and now no one can go there. Those kids were too rough with what they had."

"Hey, I was one of those kids. I love that park. It used to be a part of my home. A big part of what I think about when I remember growing up here. I didn't break it. It just needs someone to look out for it."

She turned, stomped down the stairs and gathered her backpack. "And, you're welcome."

"For what?" Joe asked.

"For painting over those cuss words." She stalked off down the street.

"Gah." Joe went back into his house. The cat sat at the top of the stair and meowed down at him. Susan's words resonated, 'It just needs someone to look out for it.'

Those were the same words his wife had said about Tabitha, when the cat had shown up at their door ten years ago. "It just needs someone to look out for it."

"Hey, Kitty," he said.

Tabitha meowed, but didn't move from her spot on the second floor landing.

"Come here, Kitty."

She crouched down to lay on her belly.

Joe set his bag of cookies on the small table in the hall, and put his hand on the dark-wood banister. He put a foot on the stair. The dust stirred and he put his other foot on the next step.

His knee ached terribly. Tabitha purred and watched him.

He took the next step and the next. The pain was excruciating.

"There's a reason I don't take use these stairs," he said.

The boards groaned under his weight. The pain in his leg nagged him to stop climbing. He stopped just short of the top and reached out to pet the cat on the head. She jumped up and darted into the bedroom.

Joe took a breath, completed the last two stairs and stood at the door to the bedroom. The dim glow of daylight shown through the gap in the mostly closed door. The green-blue plush carpet beyond was coated in cat fur and dust.

He pushed the door open.

Inside, the bed was still made, as it had been. His wife's dress lay untouched on the bed, waiting for her to slip it on for the party they'd never attended. The floor to ceiling linen curtain parted a little letting in a stream of light. Nothing had changed in nine years.

Dust layered the trinkets and jewelry on the dresser. In the corner of the dresser's mirror a picture had been wedge between the glass and the thick brown frame. He and his wife looked back smiling beside a large tree.

He turned to the closet. It was filled with dresses and shoes. A woman had touched every corner of the bedroom, and more. "This is a home someone needs to pay attention to, isn't it?" Joe said to

Tabitha.

A beeping noise came from outside the window. He pushed past the curtain to look out. Across the street a bulldozer was backing off a flatbed truck. City workers were talking with each other.

A few people from the neighborhood had gathered. They were yelling at the workers. A policeman was holding them back.

Tabitha jumped onto the bed, purring loudly. Joe limped over and sat down on his side of the bed, where he had slept for twenty years before he'd moved downstairs. Tabitha walked into his lap and settled down. He rubbed her head and stroked her back.

"I'm sorry I've neglected you."

She purred and kneaded at his thighs, pulling at his pants with her claws.

The rumble of the bulldozer took his attention. Shouting outside grew louder. Joe cocked his head sideways, realizing what was taking place outside.

"They're going to bulldoze the park? No. That isn't right. That's our park. They can't tear that down. We need to take care of it."

The cat jumped off as he stood up.

"Someone needs to do something." Joe limped back down the stairs and outside.

People were yelling, some shaking their fists at the workers. A policewoman had joined the policeman, and both were working crowd control on the gathering neighbors.

Joe spotted Susan in the group, yelling with the others. A TV cameraman mingled with the crowd, capturing everything.

The bulldozer pushed into the broken merry-go-round. The metal groaned, and twisted as it's base heaved out of the ground.

Joe gimped down the steps and across the street. The pain in his leg seemed to give him a determination to move faster. He circled around to a place where the police could not see. Using a dead bush as cover, he moved closer to the bulldozer. It backed up and pushed again at the merry-go-round.

The engine was revving, smoke poured out of its stack, the metal treads slipped on the loose dirt and dried grass. Joe hobbled up to the bulldozer and banged on the cab, trying to get the driver's attention.

"Hey! Turn it off!" He banged again.

The driver wore hearing protection and didn't take notice of Joe. Someone in the crowed pointed at him. The policeman turned and shouted something in his direction.

Joe ignored him.

One officer stepped forward and tried waving at the driver to get his attention. The other officer ran forward.

"Turn! It! Off!" Joe shouted and moved to be seen.

The bulldozer backed up and shifted its position. The scoop rammed into Joe's bad leg.

The pain seemed to explode, and Joe cried out, falling over. His head hit a rock.

The world washed between darkness and light. People gathered around him. They came in flashes; the police, a video camera, Susan.

Susan seemed to transform. Old memories stirred and blended with reality. He could see her as she had been as a little girl. See her running and playing in the park. It was a fine park then, filled with children laughing and playing.

***

He woke up in a sterile hall of an ER ward, lined with beds that were filled with people. Some were asleep, others were moaning in pain. A TV blared the local station.

An announcer said, "Dozens of angry protesters chanted for the city to stop destroying the park. One man bum-rushed the bulldozer and was sent to the hospital. That didn't slow the workers, at all. Once the man was taken away by ambulance, they plowed the whole park under."

The images on the TV showed Joe getting knocked over and an ambulance driving away. It switched to the bulldozer pushing the swings down and loading them into a truck. It cut to Susan and other neighbors shouting for them to stop.

The announcer continued, "The residents were unhappy about the park being marked for destruction so quickly, and without a hearing."

Sami, the store owner came on. "It isn't right. The children of our neighborhood are needing a place to play. Right now they have nothing, and resort to misbehaving. If the city can do it to our park, they can do it to anyone's park. Nothing is safe."

The announcer came back on. "Some on city council are looking to sell the land to developers, to ease the city's tight budget. A park lost. One man in the hospital. All for the good of the city? Back to you Roger."

A doctor came to stand between Joe and the TV. He pulled a curtain around Joe's bed.

"Ah, you're awake. I'm Doctor Reiner."

"Where am I?"

"University Hospital. ER. You took a hit to the head." "I'm fine now." Joe sat up and pulled at a wad of tape that wrapped around his hand that held a blood pressure monitor in place.

"Now wait a sec. You need to stay for observation," Doctor Reiner said.

"I need to do no such thing." Joe stood up. A hospital gown hung around him, letting air in all the places that should have been covered. "Where are my clothes?"

"You took a blow to the head and could have a serious concussion, or internal bleeding. You need an overnight stay, at the least."

"Are you saying I'm not free to go?"

The doctor paused. "No."

"Then where are my clothes."

The doctor pointed at a dresser. "In there."

"If you need me to sign anything, you'd better make it quick. I'm leaving," Joe said.

The doctor gulped. "I'll have a nurse here with papers for you to sign."

Joe pulled the curtain after the doctor, got his clothes from the dresser and changed. The nurse came in and asked him some questions, filling in a paper on a clipboard. She asked him to sign. Told him to call if he had any of the symptoms.

Joe signed and left the hospital. Outside the afternoon sun felt warm. He climbed on the next bus at the bus stop. He transferred and got off in front of this house. He went to stand where the park had been.

Growing shadows from the sinking sun cast darkness over piles of pushed dirt covered with dozer tracks. All the play equipment was gone. The benches were missing.

"They did that fast," Joe said. "This was a home that no one took care of."

He sighed, crossed the street and climbed the steps. Inside the house Tabitha watched him from the upstairs landing. She gave a small chirp of a meow.

Joe shook his head at the cat. "I've been neglecting you. I've been neglecting this house. And, the neighborhood... I've been neglecting myself."

The staircase loomed like a mountain. He put his foot down and took the first step. His knee didn't hurt. He took the next step, and still he felt fine. With each step his leg felt stronger. The pain was absent. He soon found himself marching up the stairs to the bedroom.

Once there he crossed the room. He dragged a suitcase from the floor of the closet and slung it on the bed. He popped the latch and lay it flat open.

He pulled her dresses out and folded them into the suitcase.

They all fit, so he piled her shoes on top. Once filled, he had to lean all his weight to push the suitcase closed. From under the bed he pulled out a rolling carry-on.

He scooped all the bottles and trinkets from the dresser top, dumping them into the carry-on. He opened the drawers. They were still filled with her personal things and he piled those on top. Her makeup, brushes, soaps and bottles were all dumped inside.

When everything had been loaded up, he zipped it closed and plopped it at the top of the stair. He dragged the larger suitcase off the bed and let it fall heavy to the floor. The party dress had been covered by the suitcase, and it still rested on the bed.

He picked it up, put it to his face and breathed in deep, hoping for some small scent of her. He imagined her in it, smiling and dancing. With care, he hung it up on the closet rack.

Once he'd gotten both suitcases to the bottom of the stairs he went to the phone and dialed a number.

"Hello, Homeless Foundation," a man's voice said. "Yeah. I have some women's clothes and stuff, in two suitcases. Do you pick up?"

"We do. What's your address." He gave the address and hung up.

Tabitha hunched over her bowl, eating. "What a mess," Joe said looking around.

Joe grabbed the broom and swept up the floor, dumping the dust and litter on top the heaping pile in the trash can. Next he tackled the mass of dishes in the sink.

He wiped the counters down and came across the can of spray paint. He picked it up and studied it. He shook his head and set it on the trashcan, now spilling over.

"I gotta take out the trash," he said to himself, and lifted the bag out of the can and headed out the door. Evening had settled in. A cool breeze mixed with the warm feeling of spring. He carried the trash down the steps.

Something was happening by the park. Some of his neighbors were there, and the news cameras were back, with lights on.

The can of spray paint fell out of the trash can, bounced down the steps and rolled to the middle of the sidewalk. At the bottom of the steps, Joe set down the trash, and scooped up the spray paint. He gave it a shake and felt the pellet inside rattle around.

A big black car pulled up in front of the park. The cameras pushed in close to the car. The mayor got out. He had a strong jaw. His mouth seemed stuck in a perpetual smile. Waving at the reporters on the scene, he acted like everything was great.

Joe set his jaw and crossed the street. He pushed past his neighbors, through the crowd toward the cameras.

The announcer had put a microphone in the mayor's face. "Sir, what do you have to say about this devastating scene behind us?"

The mayor flapped his palms in a placating way. "The process of city growth can be tricky to explain to every person. I assure you all, we have the best interests of our citizens in mind."

"The interests of our citizens?" Joe asked, a little surprised at how loud his voice sounded. He pressed on. "We are interested in this city because it's our home, not a place to do business, do you understand the difference? This is our home. Our kids need a place to play. We pay taxes, we elect people like you to make sure this happens. But what do we get, instead? A city that let's a playground go to waste so that it can be torn down and the land sold to the highest bidder!"

The mayor turned to an aid and muttered, "Who is this guy?"

"He's the man hit by the bulldozer today."

"Are you having trouble understanding me?" Joe asked. "Look at the spray paint all over this park. Cuss words, graphic pictures. At first I was angry about all the spray paint. I was angry at how the kids could destroy such a great park. I wondered why kids would do this. Then I realized something.

"It started when the city stopped coming here to keep the park looking nice and working. When the park fell into disrepair it was like the city said it didn't care. It was like the city was telling the kids that it doesn't care about them either. When kids think no one cares, they stop caring too. I know you care about children, don't you,

Mr. Mayor?" Joe pointed his finger at the mayor.

It was the hand that still held the spray paint can. The mayor flinched, perhaps frightened of being sprayed.

Without thinking Joe turned to the wall and sprayed a jet of yellow. The can hissed. The air was filled with the smell of paint, and fine particles of drying overspray fogged in the camera lights.

He finished spraying and stepped back. "This should help you understand," he said.

Lit by the lights of the camera crews, the yellow paint seemed to glow against the dark wall. The words were uneven, wet painted ran in long drips in places.

The words read, 'A Home Is Worth Caring For'.

"Mr. Mayor," Joe said, turning around. He had to blink at the camera lights shining in his eyes. This is our home. It needs caring for. Don't you think so?"

The crowd fell silent. The cameras and lights turned on the mayor, his eyes wide, something of a frown on his face. He hesitated just a moment before his big smile returned. He grabbed Joe and brought him close, wrapping his arm around Joe's shoulder. But careful to push joe's spray paint can down and away.

"You have misunderstood me. Really, I couldn't agree with you more," the mayor said. "I came here to tell you how disappointed I am with what has happened to this park. Our children need this park. And, I will make sure that this is the best park our city can offer."

The gathering of neighbors let out a cheer. Clapping and dancing, the crowd celebrated.

Joe held the mayor's gaze and said, "We're going to hold you to that, now."

The mayor kept on smiling through big teeth. "You have my word."

"When will new construction start?" one reporter asked. The mayor began explaining about processes and planning.

Joe pulled out of the mayor's grip and managed to push out of the crowd gathering around.

Susan was in the street, watching. "How are you doing?"

"I'm much better," Joe said.

"That was pretty hardcore. Everything you did today."

"Was it?"

"Yeah." Susan nodded.

"You were right," Joe said. "I wasn't doing anything for the neighborhood."

Susan smiled.

Sami walked up. "I just saw you on the news. You are not hurt too bad?"

"I've been hit with worse," Joe said.

"You are full of surprises today," Sami said.

"I suppose I am. Say, would you both like to come inside for some cookies?"

Susan and Sami smiled. "Sure. Why not."

Joe led them inside, past the suitcases by the door. "Are you planning a vacation?" Sami asked.

"No. In fact, I think I've been absent too long."

***

A warm Autumn sun shone on Joe, sitting on a new park bench. A squirrel climbed down a young tree, hopped across the fresh grass and took a peanut Joe had tossed on the ground.

"Look at that squirrel, mommy," said a little girl Joe knew as Julie.

She ran over from a shiny play structure at the newly rebuilt park.

Her mother, a neighbor Joe knew as Terry, joined her daughter. "Hi Joe."

"It's a fantastic afternoon for feeding squirrels," Joe said. "Would you like a try?"

Julie's grin showed a newly missing tooth. She took a peanut from his outstretched hand and tossed it on the ground near her feet. The squirrel hopped closer and picked it up. Julie squealed in delight.

The squirrel chomped on the nut and hopped back up the tree.

"Mr. Joe?" Julie said. "One of the swings is loose."

"Huh-oh," Joe said.

He pulled out his cell phone and dialed a number. "Hello. Parks and Services." the voice said. "Thomas. This is Joe Gothbury. Hey you doing?"

"Doing good, Joe. What's up?"

"It seems one of the swings at our park needs mending."

"Oh. Well, I can have a crew in that area to look at it today."

"Thanks, Thomas."

Julie and her mother's smile glowed to make the day even brighter.

It felt like a neighborhood again. The spray paint around the park had all been cleaned up, kids were playing, and the sun was shining on Joe's bench.

Discussion

At about 6,000 words, this piece of fiction was written using this guide after the first draft had been written. Being a short story, some of the stages mentioned earlier had to be left out.

Adjustments were made to some stages to keep things brief. The story accomplishes the goal of having a character progress from one state of mind to another. The following is a walk through what took place in the story, and discussion of how it relates to the stages presented in the outline.

World: A neighborhood where the park has been allowed to become run down by the city, due to budget restraints. As a result, kids have no outlet and turn to illegal acts, such as spray painting. The typical person still tries to maintain a sense of neighborhood.

The danger (while mild), is city bureaucracy that is no help. The world-joy, visiting neighbors.

Joe's desire, a nice neighborhood. His body-flaw, an arthritic knee.

His talent, he cares about the neighborhood.

The How of his flaw (how is it shown) is that he is tries to catch kids spray painting.

The Why (why he does this) he wants a nice neighborhood, but like the city, doesn't want to spend tax dollars on the park (his flaw supports the world-flaw).

Normalcy. We meet Joe in his house, and the flawed world is

introduced with cuss words, representing an unhappiness of the young people who live in this world. The world-danger, delivered through brief backstory (I know), is revealed as the bureaucracy of the city and fighting the installation of the bus stop. This backstory serves to introduce the world-danger, not motivation. We also get a hint of Joe's body flaw, his arthritic knee.

Joe goes back inside, where we get more of the city bureaucracy (world-danger) when he calls the city to report vandalism. City bureaucracy isn't a danger in the most active sense, but as an obstacle it is a danger to what is desired.

After failing to get the city to help, Joe tries to work for what he desires on his own. He get's dressed, and we see his conflicted-response with the cat. He goes outside, hoping to catch kids spray painting, as if he could. This is an example of his flawed thinking that will be made clearer.

He sees Susan for the first time, and tries to chase her. This is a conflicted-response, it is aggressive and reactionary. He fails to catch and she flees. He finds the object-catalyst, and receives the first call to action from the can of spray paint. He experiences the spray paint, but soon puts it down with the first refusal to act, and he forgets about it.

Back inside, he gets the first hint of the cataclysm from the newspaper; the destruction of the park.

On the way to the store he witnesses the world-joy; neighbors visiting. He can't have this joy because he doesn't understand that to have a nice neighborhood means being a nice neighbor. His flaw is made more apparent. We also get a better look at the park that will be destroyed.

At the store, Joe talks with the store owner Sami. Sami serves as a guide, who gives a direct second call to action; talk to the kids. Joe brushes this call off with the second refusal.

On the way home we see the cataclysm growing closer with the arrival of city workers. City workers who don't see Susan vandalizing the bus stop - a touch of the world danger shown as incompetence.

He finds Susan spray painting, this time he catches her. A seeming victory that soon becomes a great failure as she breaks away. He also experiences the climax of his physical pain.

She helps him. He begins to understand the flaw of this thinking, though he fails to relate to Susan. This scene becomes the proof of a need for change.

He goes inside, and as a hero apart, Joe reflects on Susan's words. He begins to realize he has a flaw. He attempts a misguided effort at being better to the cat, who runs away. This leads him to his old bedroom. Here he has awareness of the self. The order of stages have been changed to accommodate the story. The conflicted-response with the cat is eased.

Out the window he witnesses the growing cataclysm, and reflects on his wrong thinking. He completes the third call to action, and makes the choice to save the park. He goes to the park and tries to stop the destruction. Susan is there working on the same goal.

The sacrifice is minimal, but because he is willing to put himself in danger to protect the symbol of what he desires. The sacrifice is that he is injured.

The cataclysm strikes. The park is destroyed.

The stage 'expand the world' is shown by waking up in a hospital, where he sees other people in hospital beds. For brevity, explicit use of this stage was avoided, and the subtle implications allowed to exist on their own.

The newscast on the TV is used as a vehicle to clarify the sacrifice and loss, and to quickly get the story moving, with the announcer putting the city in a bad light as a result.

An interesting side note is that this becomes a stated assumption about the morality of the park's destruction. It also offers a hint of backstory (how city council acted quickly) to answer any lingering questions the reader might have about how a park could be destroyed without anyone finding out about it until it is too late.

Joe leaves the hospital, catches a bus and goes home to witness the aftermath at the park. Back inside his house, he is alone and reflects.

From here he gets his personal call to action. He overcomes his body-flaw and climbs the the steps to the old bedroom, pain free. He packs up all his wife's things. Through this act of rebirth he is changing how he wants to live, how he wants to see the world. This is furthered through the stage 'an active life', as Joe cleans up his house, supporting the theme that caring for your community is connected to caring for yourself.

Joe meets the mayor (the ruler of the world danger). Here Joe shows an abandonment of what he'd previously desired (a neighborhood clean of spray paint) when he applies the object catalyst to serve his own purposes. He spray paints on the wall, and in doing so he tames the world danger. The mayor befriends him. He is successful and we learn the park will be rebuilt.

On the street he meets Susan and Sami, who acknowledge his efforts through a moment of salvation. Joe invites them into his home. They accept for completion of the world-joy, neighbors visiting.

The final resolution has Joe on a park bench sharing an afternoon with neighbors. He learns of a broken swing and calls the city.

This shows him with what he desires (a neighborhood), using new skills and the tamed danger (he can call the city). This hints that being the best one can be requires ongoing effort, which is the point when presenting character development as a spiritual transformation.

Beginning

Normalcy

First Call to Action

First Call Refused

Introduction Of Cataclysm

Normal No More

Middle

Introduction of the Guide

Second Call to Action

Second Refusal

Cataclysm Approaches

Cataclysm Not Avoided

Expand The World

Conflict with the Guide

Proof of Need for Change

The Hero Apart

Third Call to Action

*Revelation

  The Unsure Self

  The Three Quiet Resolutions

  The Hero Perfected

Awareness of Self

Resolution with the Guide

World-Joy

End

Sacrifice

  Decision To Sacrifice

  The Sacrifice

The Cataclysm Strikes

Aftermath

  The Hero Alone

  The Hero Reflects

  An Active Life

Rebirth

  Putting the Object to Use

  World Danger Tamed

  Overcoming the Body

Salvation

Final Resolution

143